"Greg Gilbert is a world-class expositor. ([ ]
preaching for nearly twelve years.) *The Epic Story of the Bible will* [ ]
ize your ability to grasp the sweeping, soaring narrative that centers—from
Genesis to Revelation—on Jesus the King. Read and marvel."

   Matt Smethurst, Lead Pastor, River City Baptist Church,
   Richmond, Virginia; Editor, The Gospel Coalition; author, *Deacons*
   and *Before You Share Your Faith*

"I sometimes worry when we try to identify the Bible's major theme or core
message since the Bible is more like a rich ecosystem of themes working
together to offer us a picture of God and his glory. However, in this very
readable book, Greg Gilbert brings together important biblical themes to
help Christians, whether new to or seasoned in the faith, understand God's
word. With a good command of biblical themes, helpful illustrations, and
personal anecdotes along the way, Gilbert shows himself to be a clear and
accessible guide for God's people."

   Mark Jones, Pastor, Faith Vancouver Presbyterian Church, British
   Columbia, Canada

"This is a resource that equips us to be better Bible readers and infuses
delight in God's redemptive work. What a gift! Greg Gilbert skillfully leads
us over the terrain of Scripture, helping us grasp its sweeping story and
biblical themes. It will be a great asset to the training work of churches and
organizations in how to study the Bible and rejoice in our Savior and King."

   Taylor Turkington, Director, BibleEquipping.org

"I am thrilled about Greg Gilbert's guide to exploring the story of the Bible.
This provides the essentials we need to get started—an overview of the Bible's
intricate and epic storyline, along with its central themes. I am eager to see
how this helps many engage the Bible with eagerness and understanding."

   Drew Hunter, Teaching Pastor, Zionsville Fellowship, Zionsville,
   Indiana; author, *Made for Friendship*

The Epic Story of the Bible

The Epic Story
of the Bible

How to Read and Understand God's Word

Greg Gilbert

::: CROSSWAY®

WHEATON, ILLINOIS

Library of Congress Cataloging-in-Publication Data

Names: Gilbert, Greg, 1977– author.
Title: The epic story of the Bible : how to read and understand God's word / Greg Gilbert.
Description: Wheaton, Illinois : Crossway, 2022. | Includes bibliographical references and index.
Identifiers: LCCN 2022001607 (print) | LCCN 2022001608 (ebook) | ISBN 9781433573279 (trade paperback) | ISBN 9781433573286 (pdf) | ISBN 9781433573293 (mobi) | ISBN 9781433573309 (epub)
Subjects: LCSH: Bible—Introductions.
Classification: LCC BS475.3 .G555 2022 (print) | LCC BS475.3 (ebook) | DDC 220.6/1—dc23/eng/20220321
LC record available at https://lccn.loc.gov/2022001607
LC ebook record available at https://lccn.loc.gov/2022001608

Contents

Introduction

AS THE PLANE DESCENDED toward the city, I didn't see any mountains out the window. At some level, this was disappointing, because that was why I'd come in the first place. But on the other hand, when your plane is landing in a driving rainstorm, your primary emotion usually isn't disappointment of any kind but rather just relief to feel the wheels land, the brakes kick in, and the plane slow down enough that your body slumps back down in the seat again. I dropped my head back and grinned. For a year, I'd been planning this trip, and now I was here, in Kathmandu, Nepal, about to set off on a two-week trek to the South Base Camp of Sagarmatha, better known as Mount Everest.

I was excited, and more than a little nervous. For whatever reason, I've always been fascinated by mountains, and through the years I've seized every opportunity I could to be in and among them—skiing the Rockies in Colorado, hiking the Green Mountains in Vermont and the White Mountains in New Hampshire and Maine, even spending a week in the utter wilderness of Alaska at a working gold mine, just for the fun of it. So when the time and opportunity opened up, I jumped at the chance to trek into the tallest, most dramatic mountain range in the world, the Himalayas, and set foot at the base of the tallest mountain on Earth. That's where the excitement came from.

The fear came from reading online about other people's experiences on this Base Camp trek. For the most part, what I had signed up to do was relatively easy and safe—no technical climbing, no crampons or elite winter gear or oxygen tanks required. This was Everest for Dummies for sure, not *Everest* the movie! And yet, it wasn't a walk in the park, either. By the end of the trek, we would finally top out at an elevation of 18,200 feet, high enough (I was told) that if a helicopter took you there immediately from sea level, you'd be unconscious within fifteen minutes due to the lack of oxygen. Of course we were planning to do all kinds of acclimatization, but still, I'd read the blogs. It was no sure thing that those measures would work for any given person. You can do everything right to get yourself ready for high altitudes, only to get halfway up into the Himalayas and realize suddenly—and sometimes catastrophically—that your body just doesn't have the necessary hardware. Your brain begins to swell, your lungs fill up with fluid, and within a few hours you find yourself being medevacked back to a Kathmandu hospital—that is, if the weather on the mountain is conducive to a rescue. Beyond that, there were other dangers, too: falls, broken bones, getting knocked off the mountain by a yak—you know, the usual kinds of things I have to think about in Louisville, Kentucky!

So as the plane pulled up to the gate at the Tribhuvan International Airport, Nepal's only international airport, I pulled my passport out of my backpack and turned to the page where my Nepali visa was pasted. I checked all my information again: name was spelled correctly, dates correct, vaccinations all up to date—a bunch of facts I'm sure I had confirmed probably a hundred times on this flight already, but excitement makes you do funny things. I shoved the passport back into its special pocket on my backpack and locked it in. I'd read on several websites that you can't be too careful in the Kathmandu airport terminal. Besides the normal threats like theft of money and documents, I'd also been told of a terrifying scam in which the customs agents will sometimes "neglect" to stamp your visa as you pass through, and then when you show it to the next set of agents, you're immediately placed under arrest for "invalid documentation." From there, the scam is to get as much money out of you as possible. You're given a choice—you can either spend a month in prison, or you can pay an exorbitant fee to be driven over the course of a few days to a bureaucratic office to "get it sorted out." If you choose the latter, you pay up front and then—unbeknownst to you, of course—you'll be told at various points along the way that it's going to cost you even more money to get any further. Finally, after a week or so and a few thousand dollars, you return triumphantly to Kathmandu Airport with your newly "sorted out" visa.

Was any of that actually true? I have no idea. But you better believe I watched the customs agent like a hawk as he examined my passport. And I got that stamp, baby!

Fully sorted out diplomatically, I walked across the terminal to the pickup area, scanned the drivers holding signs with various people's names on them, and finally found my guy, complete with a bright blue hat that read "Ultimate Expeditions." Once in the van with two or three others, I finally relaxed and let myself revel in what was happening. I was in Nepal, about to hike to Mount

Everest—not *up* it, no, but even hiking *to* Everest, I figured, was pretty amazing.

The plan for that evening was pretty straightforward. The driver would take me and the other passengers to our hotel, we'd have a little while to rest in our rooms, and then we'd gather in the hotel restaurant for dinner and what was being called "the briefing," a presentation in which our guide would explain, before we ever took the first step, what we were about to experience.

The briefing wasn't long. The guide started by showing us a video depicting an aerial flyby of the trail we were going to hike, then a fly-around of the whole Everest massif—a U-shaped trio of mountains including Lohtse (the fourth-highest mountain in the world), Nuptse (the twenty-second), and of course Everest itself. He told us about the places we'd visit through the course of the trek and explained the fascinating aspects of each one—the Lukla airport, commonly said to be the most dangerous in the world; the mountainside town of Namche Bazaar, gateway to the high Himalayas and home to the highest and remotest Irish pub on the planet; the little village of Khumjung, which displays what the monks there claim is a real yeti scalp but which the villagers themselves will tell you is just a yak butt; Tengboche Monastery, built over a hundred years ago on a ridge that provides hikers with breathtaking panoramic views of the Khumbu region; and Base Camp itself, a tiny village of brightly colored tents huddled at the foot of the massive Mount Everest and inhabited by the tiny group of (let's be honest) slightly crazy people who would be headed to the summit on the very days we were there.

I listened with utter fascination not only to my guide's descriptions of these fantastic places I was soon to see, but also to the smaller asides he made throughout the meeting. "When we land at Lukla, notice how the plane doesn't really descend; the runway is at ten thousand feet, so the plane will just kind of *hit* it." "You need to eat carbs and drink water like crazy, because they help with acclimatization." "When we're passing through the rhododendron forests, look for children hiding up in the trees; it's a game to them, and they like to give flowers to tourists who notice them." "Respect the Sherpas who pass by us with enormous loads on their backs; essentially every item needed for human survival in the high Himalayas has to be brought in on foot, and to huff it all in on their backs is how these people make a living."

When the briefing was finished, I was stoked for the trek to start. I didn't sleep all night. I just lay in the bed with images and words from that meeting rolling around in my mind's eye. It was an incredible presentation, hyping the trip and giving vital information. But I'll be honest—looking back on it now, I had no idea just how important the briefing would turn out to be for shaping the entire experience. What the guide conveyed—the information, the maps, the geography, the images, the history and cultural background of the region—threw the entire two-week trek into 3D for me. At any given moment, I *knew where I was* on the trail, and I knew where we were going. When we got to Namche Bazaar, I understood why that town was so important, and I was able to appreciate it all the more because of it. When I saw a sign for Khumjung, I smiled because I remembered, "Oh, this is where I'm supposed to look for the yeti scalp!" Even more, I avoided making mistakes: I ate carbs and drank water; I made way for heavy-burdened Sherpas and took a silent moment to respect them for making human civilization possible this far up in the Himalaya. The briefing hadn't been long, but it had been crucial. It changed and deepened and enriched my experience of the Himalayas in ways I never would have guessed.

———

You probably didn't pick up this particular book because you have an interest in mountaineering. But I tell you that story about the briefing in that rain-pelted hotel in Kathmandu because that's essentially what I'm aiming to do with this book—give you a briefing about what you're going to see, what you're going to experience, what you should look for and look *out* for as you set off on the long trek of reading the entire Bible.

A trek. That's exactly what it is when you decide to read the entire Bible. After all, it's sixty-six different books with thirty-some different authors, written over the course of a millennium and a half. And it's long—almost 1,200 chapters and three-quarters of a million words, meaning that if you decided to read the entire thing aloud, all at once, it would take you just under three days to do it—about seventy hours and forty minutes if you're an average-speed reader. Moreover, the Bible contains many different kinds of literature. There's poetry and narrative, lists and genealogies, biographies and law codes and prophecies and sermons and open letters and personal letters and even something called "apocalyptic." It's no wonder so many people feel bewildered when they open up the Bible and attempt to read it. Actually, most people do pretty well through Genesis and the first part of Exodus. But once Exodus starts launching into Old Testament Law and doesn't really come up for air for a book and a half, that's when many people start thinking, "Wow, life's gotten busy! Maybe I'll give this another try next week . . . or month . . . or year."

I think the key to reading the Bible, though, is to understand that all of those authors and books—all 1,189 chapters of them—are actually working together to tell one overarching, mind-blowing story about God's action to save human beings from their high-handed rebellion against him, and from the effects and consequences of that rebellion. And the thing is, the story of how he did that is quite literally *epic* in its scope and its sweep. Wars between angels rage in the spiritual realm, while on earth kingdoms rise and fall, empires clash, cities are built and destroyed, priests perform sacrifices, and prophets point their bony fingers to the future. And in the end, a great throne is toppled and a great crown falls to the ground, only to be given finally to one thirty-year-old man—a subjugated peasant from a conquered nation—whom God enthrones over the entire world as the one who alone can and does offer mercy to rebels. If there's ever been an epic story told in the history of mankind, this one is it!

Maybe you've read epic stories before, stories so sweeping in their enormity, in the comprehensiveness of the world they build, that you feel not so much like you're reading the story from the outside as that you are actually a part of it. And when it comes to an end, when you get to the last chapter, you hesitate to read it because you know you're about to have to leave this world you've been so immersed in. I felt that way when I read Tolkien's *The Lord of the Rings* for the first time. I—a self-assured, cocky college freshman—cried when the book was over, because the world Tolkien had created, the story he wove, had captured my imagination and pulled me entirely into it. Its themes, its rhythms, its poetry and prose, the arc of despair giving way to hope—by the end, I wasn't just *reading* that story; I was *in* it, living it, experiencing it.

Imagine, though, if I had read *The Lord of the Rings* like most people tend to read the Bible. Imagine if I'd taken *Rings*, opened it to a random place and read the first sentence or two my eyes landed on. Sure, there might have been some beauty in it; I might have been able to "get something out of it" immediately; there might have been some "life application" to be had. But that kind of reading would have been empty, vacant, and lifeless compared to reaching that same paragraph with the full weight of the story behind it. Or imagine if I read *The Lord of the Rings* with the main questions in my mind being "What does this mean for me? How can this help me be a better person? What lessons can I learn from this?" Again, you might wind up learning some important things reading the book like that, but you'd be fundamentally misunderstanding the story's aim. You'd be reading it in a fundamentally self-centered and far too self-aware way, when the aim of the story is really to sweep you away in the narrative, to carry you along in a story in which *you* are not the starring character but in which the idea is to fall in love with *other* characters. That's how epic stories are meant to be read—not as tiny little morality tales, but as horizon-busting, eye-bugging, world-broadening, even life-shaping *experiences*.

One more example: imagine reading *The Lord of the Rings* out of order. You pick it up, flip over to Rivendell for a moment, then hop over to Mordor before slamming back into the Shire; maybe you decide to read half of Tom Bombadil's song the next day, and then end it up with a little bit of Shelob's Lair. Now, if you've read the story from start to finish once or twice already, that might be lots of fun—reading your favorite parts over again. But it's no way to understand the story of *The Lord of the Rings*! And it's no way to understand the epic story of the Bible either, even though the hop-skip-and-jump method of reading is the one I think most Christians try to employ most of the time. When my daughter was about six years old, I asked what she learned in Sunday school one Sunday, and she replied, "Abraham died for Jesus's sins on the ark, and then King Josiah raised him from the dead!" If you read the Bible the way most of us tend to—and in the order most of us tend to—you might be thinking that's actually not a terrible summary of the story!

But of course we know it *is* terrible, don't we? That's not the story, and that's not how the Bible should be read—not out of order, not as a bunch of little morality tales, certainly not with ourselves and our concerns at the center of our consciousness of it—but rather as the sweepingly epic story of God's heroic rescue of mankind from our deadly rebellion against him. That's what I hope this book will help you learn to do.

You can think of reading the Bible as a trek through the Himalayas and this book as the briefing meeting, just like the one I had in Kathmandu, before you set out on the trek. My hope here is to do several things.[1] I want to introduce you to some of the things you're going to see and experience as you read the entire Bible. I want to point out some things you should watch for—beautiful things that you might otherwise miss and dangerous things that you should be on guard against. I want to tell you

---

1   I preached on this topic at T4G 2020. Text of the full sermon is available "A T4G 2020 Sermon: What Is and Isn't the Gospel" on the 9Marks website, https://www .9marks.org/.

about the various kinds of terrain you're going to traverse, that is, the different genres of literature you're going to be reading, and I want to help you begin to understand the unique skills and rules you're going to need to keep in mind in order to traverse that terrain without, well, breaking your literary ankles. But maybe above all, I want to get you excited for the trek. I want you not to be able to sleep tonight, knowing what's waiting for you out there. I want your heart to be full of expectation and eagerness for what you're about to see as you begin to read and experience this grand, epic story that is the Bible.

So let's start the briefing . . . by getting some basic facts about the trail.

1

What the Bible Is, and
Where It Came From

NEPAL IS A COUNTRY in South Asia, situated just to the north-east of India in the heart of the Himalayan Mountains. It's not a large country—only about the size of Arkansas—but it boasts a population of almost 30 million. The flag of Nepal is the only one in the world that's not in the shape of a quadrilateral. Instead, it looks like two triangles fused together and is meant to represent the mountains and their importance to the history and culture of the nation. The vast majority of the people are Hindu in religion and culture, and most of the rest are Buddhist. The most popular dish—eaten by some of the people for all three meals—is a lentil and rice mixture called *dal bhat*. Both hearty and cheap, it has the benefit of leaving both the stomach and the wallet feeling relatively full. Nepal also boasts the world's largest elevation change, from just above sea level at the Tarai Plains to the highest point on the entire planet, Everest's 29,032-foot summit. Strangely, Nepal's clocks aren't set to any normal time zone; my home in Louisville wasn't nine or ten hours off, but rather *nine hours and forty-five minutes off*! I never learned exactly why that is, but so much for trying to figure out what time it was back home.

All these facts I learned in the days and weeks running up to my trip to Nepal, and also during the twenty-two-hour series of flights I had to take to get there. In one way or another, all of those facts were important for the trip I was about to take. They taught me something about the nation's culture, its history, and its geography. Just by knowing a few basic and interesting facts about Nepal, I was able to orient myself to what I was about to experience. I knew, for example, that *dal bhat* was not to be missed. I knew I'd be encountering Hindu and Buddhist religious practices, and sometimes even a syncretistic mixture of the two of them. And I knew it would be entirely fruitless for me to schedule phone calls with anybody back in the States.

Anytime you're about to visit a new country or set off on a journey, it's a good idea to get some basic facts about the place you're going. What's its character? Its history? Where did it come from and what are you likely to encounter there? Without a doubt the same thing is true when you're setting off on a journey of reading through the entire Bible. After all, for all of us here in the twenty-first century, we are headed to a time and place that is almost completely foreign to us. The customs are different, the history is largely unknown to us, and even the kinds of literature and writing that make it up can strike us as unfamiliar and downright strange.

So before we dive into the deep end, let's take a few moments to get familiar with the Bible at the highest level—not its storyline;

we'll get to that in the next chapter. Let's look at its even more basic structure, the most fundamental facts about what it is and where it came from.

At its most fundamental level—before we even get to what Christians believe about it being the word of God—the Bible is a collection of sixty-six different books written by thirty-some different authors over the span of some fifteen hundred years, the last of which was completed about two thousand years ago. It was written in three different languages—Hebrew, Greek, and Aramaic—and in the English Standard Version it contains 757,349 words, about 30 percent longer than Tolstoy's *War and Peace*. If you sat down to read the Bible from cover to cover at a normal out-loud reading pace, it would take you just under seventy-two hours to do.

In reality, to call the sixty-six books of the Bible "books" is a little misleading. For the most part, they're not books in the sense that this book you're reading is a *book*. Some of them are, to be sure, but many of the books of the Bible are . . . other things. They're poems or letters or sermons or songbooks or collections of sayings. Though that may sound daunting at first—especially if we're trying to learn how to read the Bible as one sweeping story—I think this variety imbues the Bible with an extra layer of fascination and mystery.

In 2007, author Max Brooks wrote a fictional work called *World War Z: An Oral History of the Zombie War*. It wasn't your normal everyday novel, running from start to finish with prose written from the standpoint of a third-person author or even from the standpoint of one of the main characters. Instead, Brooks told his story by switching back and forth between various literary types—a journal entry, then an email, then a list of supplies, and on and on. It made for a fascinating story because as a reader you constantly had to be reading between the lines in order to catch the deepest themes of the story. In many ways the Bible works in the same way. Some of its story is told in prose, but that prose is then augmented by prophecies and songs, letters and memoirs. And as the story builds and grows, its themes rolling and swelling forward, you see it come to life in a way you never would if it were a straight-line prose narrative.

Of course, one of the benefits Max Brooks had in writing his *World War Z* was that he had 100 percent authority to include in his book anything he thought would push the story forward. If he wanted to include a grocery list, in went the grocery list! Email? Done! If he'd even wanted to include something utterly unrelated to the story—a birthday card from his mom—who would have been able to tell him not to? (An editor. That's who. But that's not my point.) My point is that Max Brooks, as the singular author of his book, got to decide what to put in his book. If that's true, then who exactly made those decisions when it came to the Bible? Who decided that *this* prophetic book should go into it, but not that one? These four accounts of the life of Jesus, but not that one? This letter, but not those over there?

The answer to that question isn't as easy as it is for some other books. For *World War Z*, the answer is five words long: Max Brooks and his editor. For most books, in fact, the answer is about that simple. But for the Bible, not so much. The trouble, though, is that people really *want* there to be such a simple answer to the question of who got to decide what to put in the Bible. Surely, they think, there must have been a council of bishops at some point—or maybe a Roman emperor—who just decided which books would be part of the Bible and which would not. And of course the dark undercurrent of that thought is that, surely, they must have made that decision in order to hide other books that would be detrimental to their plans—whatever those plans might have been!

That was basically the story Dan Brown told in his 2003 book *The Da Vinci Code*. I'll be honest; I liked that book. I have liked most of Dan Brown's novels because I'm a sucker for page-turning, mostly mindless action stories with just enough faux highbrow intellectualism to make me think I'm learning something. Guilty as charged! What set *The Da Vinci Code* apart from Brown's other books, though, was that so many people around the world seemed to forget that it was *fiction*. People (and news organizations, embarrassingly) started acting as if its central "truth"—that Jesus survived, got married, had children, and even had living descendants—was actually true. And a big part of that story, necessary to it in fact, was the idea that the Bible as we know it was a central part of the conspiracy. Here's how the story went: Powerful early Christians knew that Jesus didn't actually die on the cross, rise from the dead, and ascend into heaven; they knew that he really settled down into domestic life, had some kids, and lived well into old age. But of course those "facts" would be unfortunate for their project of using the fictional Jesus they'd constructed to build a new religion and make themselves wealthy and powerful. So they just buried the facts. They picked a few books that backed up their fictional account of Jesus, suppressed other writings that undermined it, and presented their "Bible" to the world: "Here it is! Behold the canon!"

Dan Brown actually places the blame for all of this at the feet of Emperor Constantine; the bishops were just his cronies apparently. Here's one account Brown has his characters give of where the Bible came from:

> "Who chose which gospels to include?" Sophie asked.
>
> "Aha!" Teabing burst in with enthusiasm. "The fundamental irony of Christianity! The Bible, as we know it today, was collated by the pagan Roman emperor Constantine the Great."[1]

Of course that's absolute historical nonsense; it's fiction, as much fiction as the rest of Brown's book. But to be fair to him, at least Brown says, on the very first page of his work, that his book is fiction. The real tragedy is that so many people—even scholars—have embraced this sneering-emperor-and-his-cronies account of how the Bible was put together as *fact*. That's a tragedy because it's just not true. So if it wasn't some group of people deciding which books to include and which to reject, how then did it happen? Let's start with the Old Testament. Where did it come from?

The idea of a list of writings that would be accepted by the Jewish people as authoritative undoubtedly began with the tablets of stone on which God wrote the Ten Commandments and then gave to the people. Exodus 31:18 tells us that these tablets were "written with the finger of God," and therefore were treated with the utmost respect and reverence. Moses says in Deuteronomy 10:5 that he placed the tablets inside the ark of the covenant, which God had commanded him to make. As time passed, other writings from Jewish leaders were afforded this same level of re-

---

1 Dan Brown, *The Da Vinci Code* (New York, Anchor Books, 2003), 303–4.

spect. Moses's writings were placed beside the ark of the covenant (Deut. 31:24–26), and Joshua—Moses's successor—is said to have written his account of the conquest of the Promised Land "in the book of the Law of God" (Josh. 24:26). Over the centuries, other people in Israel's history were recognized as ones who spoke the very words of God, and their words too were included among those writings which were seen as absolutely authoritative. So Samuel wrote his words and "laid it up before the Lord" (1 Sam. 10:25); David's acts were written down in the chronicles of three "seers" or prophets (1 Chron. 29:29); and the Lord himself commanded Jeremiah to write down his words in a book (Jer. 30:2).

Of course there were debates among Jewish scholars about whether certain books deserved to be included in this "canon"— or standard—of authoritative books. The books of Esther and Song of Songs, for instance, didn't even mention God's name; should they be included as authoritative Scripture for the nation? What about Proverbs and Ecclesiastes, whose wisdom seems so counterintuitive at times? (Should we answer a fool according to his folly, or not [Prov. 26:4–5]? Is there really nothing better than to eat and drink and find enjoyment in our work [Eccles. 2:24], and do we really want to teach our children that "money solves everything [Eccles. 10:19]?). By about 435 BC, though, the canon of the Old Testament seems to have solidified and the debates to have ended. After that date (the approximate date of the book of Malachi), nothing more was added to the canon. It was closed.[2]

2 Several ancient sources attest to the closing of the canon after 435 BC. First Maccabees 4, for example, acknowledges several times that at the time of the Maccabean revolt, there were no prophets in Israel and had not been any for quite some time. Josephus, writing his *Against Apion* at about the turn of the first century AD, said that although

Most importantly, the New Testament documents make it clear that Jesus himself left no question that the canon of the Old Testament was well-defined and closed. In several places he even says things that embrace—in an exclusive kind of way—the entire collection of books. For example, in Luke 24:44–45, Jesus teaches his disciples that everything that had happened to him was the fulfillment of Old Testament prophecy : "'These are my words that I spoke to you while I was still with you, that everything written about me in the Law of Moses and the Prophets and the Psalms must be fulfilled.' Then he opened their minds to understand the Scriptures."

There are a couple of interesting things to see here. First, notice that "the Scriptures" is synonymous with what Jesus calls "the Law of Moses and the Prophets and the Psalms." By the time Jesus was born, the Hebrew Scriptures were regularly talked about as having three divisions—the Law (*Torah*), the Prophets (*Nevi'im*), and the Writings (*Ketuvim*). So ingrained had that division become, in fact, that a single word was invented to refer to the whole collection; using the first letter of each of those Hebrew words, the whole canon was called the *TaNaKh*. What's interesting about Jesus's words in Luke 24:44 is that he refers to all three of those divisions. True, he doesn't specifically mention the Writings like he does the Law and the Prophets, but the Psalms were the first book of the Writings and therefore probably could stand for the

---

other histories of the Jewish people had been lately written, none of those had been "deemed worthy of equal credit with the earlier records, because of the failure of the exact succession of the prophets." Maccabees, Josephus, rabbinic literature, and even the Qumran community all agree: after 435 BC and the prophecy of Malachi, no other books were added by the Jewish people to their canon of authoritative Scripture.

whole division. See the point? Jesus himself recognized the accepted canon of Old Testament Scripture, embracing all three divisions of the entire Tanakh.

This fact is underscored further by something Jesus said in Luke 11:51. At that particular moment, Jesus is launching an absolute scorcher of a diatribe against the Jewish Pharisees and teachers of the Law. One of the lawyers interrupts him and complains that Jesus is insulting him and his kind. Undeterred, Jesus doubles down, declaring that this lawyer and the other Jewish leaders will be held accountable by God for all the blood of the prophets that they have spilled since the beginning of time. Here's what he says:

> Therefore also the Wisdom of God said, "I will send them prophets and apostles, some of whom they will kill and persecute," so that the blood of all the prophets, shed from the foundation of the world, may be charged against this generation, from the blood of Abel to the blood of Zechariah, who perished between the altar and the sanctuary. Yes, I tell you, it will be required of this generation. (Luke 11:49–51)

Now obviously this isn't the main point we should take away from what Jesus says here, but look carefully at that phrase "from the blood of Abel to the blood of Zechariah." What does that mean? The key to understanding it is to know that the Jewish people ordered the books of the Old Testament differently than we do, the most important difference being that the very last book of the Hebrew Scriptures was not Malachi but 2 Chronicles, the end of which tells the story of the martyrdom of Zechariah, son of Jehoiada the priest. But there's the kicker: Zechariah was not the last prophet to be killed *chronologically speaking*. That was Uriah some three hundred years later, whose story is told in Jeremiah 26. But *canonically speaking*, Jesus's words embrace the entire Tanakh as the Jews ordered it—from the blood of Abel the first martyr in Genesis 4:8 to the blood of Zechariah the last martyr written about in 2 Chronicles 24:20–22. Again, the point is clear: by the time of Jesus, the Hebrew Scriptures were a well-established collection of authoritative writings, composed of three well-recognized divisions ordered from Genesis to 2 Chronicles. And what is more, Jesus *endorsed* that collection from start to finish as being the written word of God.[3]

So we know that the Old Testament was formed over the centuries through a process of the Jewish people recognizing books that came with prophetic authority and were in accord with what they knew to be the written word of God (beginning with the tablets and the words of Moses himself). The New Testament was formed through a similar process, but faster. From the very beginning, the early Christians knew that Jesus had given a special authority to the apostles—those who were eyewitnesses of his resurrection and had been *personally* called and sent by him—to speak his words to the fledgling church. This knowledge came from an occasion just before his death during which Jesus specifically gave his apostles this kind of authority. John eventually recorded what happened:

> [Jesus said,] "I still have many things to say to you, but you cannot bear them now. When the Spirit of truth comes, he will guide you into all the truth, for he will not speak on his

---

3 For more information about the formation of the biblical canon, see F. F. Bruce, *The Canon of Scripture* (Downers Grove, IL: IVP Academic, 2018).

own authority, but whatever he hears he will speak, and he will declare to you the things that are to come. He will glorify me, for he will take what is mine and declare it to you. All that the Father has is mine; therefore I said that he will take what is mine and declare it to you." (John 16:12–15)

That's a really extraordinary event, isn't it? Jesus promises his apostles that once he has risen from the dead and ascended to heaven, he will send the Holy Spirit to speak Jesus's words to his apostles, and then they in turn will (presumably) speak it to others. In other words, Jesus is giving his apostles a special authority and commission to speak in his name, and enjoining those who would follow him (Christians!) to accept what they say as his very words. As the years passed following the resurrection, it's clear that the apostles took this commission of authority very seriously; they believed *and asserted* that what they were writing was Scripture. So for example, in 1 Corinthians 14:37 Paul says, "If anyone thinks that he is a prophet, or spiritual, he should acknowledge that the things I am writing to you are a command of the Lord." In 1 Thessalonians 2:13 he says of his own preaching and writing, "And we also thank God constantly for this, that when you received the word of God, which you heard from us, you accepted it not as the word of men but as what it really is, the word of God." In Revelation 1:3, John makes a similar claim for his own book: "Blessed is the one who reads aloud the words of this prophecy, and blessed are those who hear, and who keep what is written in it, for the time is near."

It wasn't just that the apostles regarded their *own* writings as authoritative, either; they also recognized the writings of the other apostles as being Scripture. The most interesting example of this is also the most amusing. In 2 Peter 3:15–16, Peter writes this:

> And count the patience of our Lord as salvation, just as our beloved brother Paul also wrote to you according to the wisdom given him, as he does in all his letters when he speaks in them of these matters. There are some things in them that are hard to understand, which the ignorant and unstable twist to their own destruction, as they do the other Scriptures.

The funny thing here, of course, is that Peter himself recognizes that Paul's writing can be hard to understand sometimes. But the most important phrase Peter uses when talking about people twisting Paul's writings is "as they do the other Scriptures." The *other* Scriptures! In other words, Peter puts Paul's writings on the same level as the Old Testament canon.

Do you see the point of this? The development of the New Testament canon was never a matter of any group of Christians sitting down before a table of hundreds and hundreds of documents and having to (or getting to) choose which ones would be included in the collection. Rather, the early Christians knew that Jesus had specially authorized his exclusive group of apostles to speak for him, and those apostles repeatedly asserted their own acceptance of that authority. So when a church received a letter or account of the life of Jesus that could be authenticated as genuinely written by one of those apostles (or, as in the case of Luke for example, so close an associate of one of the apostles that it could basically be said that the author was speaking *for* that apostle), and when its contents could be seen to line up with what Christians already knew to be true and to be of general benefit to Christians across the world, those letters or accounts of Jesus's life were accepted as authoritative.

To be sure, there were debates about what belonged and what didn't. Challenges arose when a book was put forward for acceptance, or an accepted book was singled out as not belonging. In those cases, the early Christians had to do some careful thinking, and over the years they informally and organically developed a series of tests by which they would determine if a particular document should be accepted as part of the canon. The four tests were: apostolicity, antiquity, universality, and orthodoxy. All four of those tests were actually written down in the late second century in a document known as "the Muratorian Canon," but they were in use long before that. The point of the Muratorian Canon is not to suggest those tests as a new method, but rather to say, essentially, "This is how we've been thinking through this for a long time." Simply put, the test of *apostolicity* meant that the early Christians were recognizing the authority Jesus had given to his apostles to speak his word; if you weren't an apostle (or at least a close associate of one), then your book didn't have a snowball's chance in the Mediterranean region of being accepted. *Antiquity* was similar; if your book was written, say, in the late third century, then it wouldn't be accepted because all the apostles were dead and gone by then. *Universality* meant that books of a very specific nature, or books that were used only by a small subsection of the universal church, weren't eligible for inclusion; the words Jesus would speak to his apostles for use by the church would be useful for the *whole* church. Finally, *orthodoxy* meant that the writings included in the canon would have to match up with what Christians already knew to be true about Jesus. For example, Christians knew beyond a shadow of doubt that Jesus rose from the dead, so any book (even if it had, say, Peter's name on it) that claimed otherwise would be immediately rejected.

So you see? There was no council of bishops or imperial edict that arbitrarily, much less maliciously, decided which books would be in the canon. The early Christians simply *received* the words of the apostles as authoritative, just as Jesus had told them to in that moment recorded in John 16, and then when challenges or questions arose from one direction or another, they used very well thought through criteria—apostolicity, antiquity, universality, and orthodoxy—to adjudicate those questions. I mean, stop and think about it for a minute: If it were up to you, what other criteria would you use? Given what Jesus said in John 16, can you think of a better way to determine which books you would accept as authoritative than what they came up with? "We will receive those books which are written by apostles or their secretaries, which are of benefit to the whole of Jesus's people throughout the world, and which match up with what we already know to be true." That's what they said, and if you ask me, that seems like a pretty good and reasonable set of tests.

Ultimately, Christians believe that the Bible is the written word of God. There are many reasons for that belief, among which is the Bible's own claim to that status. The apostles' repeated assertions that their own writings, and those of the other apostles, carry that kind of authority falls into that category. So does John's claim about his Revelation, and his unapologetic declaration in 1 John 4:6 that "we are from God. Whoever knows God listens to us; whoever is not from God does not listen to us." Most importantly, though, Christians believe the Bible is the word of God because Jesus believed that. As we've seen, from start to finish he—the resurrected one—endorsed the Old Testament and authorized the New. That's why we believe it.

But here's the thing: even if you're not a Christian (yet), and even if you're not ready to go all the way and agree that the Bible is the word of God, don't be too quick to reject it. Even when considered to be just historical artifacts, the collection of books we're talking about here is extraordinary. Sixty-six books, thirty-five authors, fifteen hundred years—all (I hope you'll come to see) collectively and harmoniously telling one epic story of God's relationship with humankind, a story that culminated in a single saving act so unexpected, so breathtaking, that it permanently changed the course of human history.

That's the story you're about to be immersed in as you begin this journey of reading the Bible. It won't be short; it won't be easy; but it will be worth the trek. So let's take a look at the trail ahead.

2

The Trail Ahead

The Grand Storyline of the Bible

IN THE MONTHS leading up to my trek through the Khumbu Region of the Himalayas, I absolutely wore Google Earth out. I love Google Earth; I love how you can fly over cities and areas of the planet that you've never seen before, and it's almost like you're there. I've flown over the Rockies and the Alps, through the Roman Forum and across the great cities of Europe and Asia. I've flown low across the Serengeti and up the slopes of Kilimanjaro. Once I even decided to traverse Antarctica, and (like the intrepid explorers of old, of course) I skimmed, in the perfect comfort of my living room, clear and clean across that bleak continent's expanse. It took me about a minute and a half, even factoring in a catastrophic wrong turn occasioned by a less-than-expert-level proficiency in Google Earth's flight controls.

But even if Antarctica gave me some trouble, I absolutely *mastered* the Khumbu Region of Nepal, flying over the route of my coming trek again and again and again. The course started at the airport in the little village of Lukla in the southern foothills of the Himalayas, and from there it wound down several miles and a couple thousand feet of elevation to a village called Phakding. Flying in my Google Earth simulated airplane, I could turn north from there, up the Khumbu Valley to the last true outpost of civilization—the town of Namche Bazaar, nestled in a semicircular pattern against the side of a mountain, elevation 11,291 feet. Soaring over Namche, I could look across the valley to the monastery of Tengboche, balanced on a ridge that juts out over the valley and backdropped by the stunning southern slope of Mount Lhotse, Everest's companion and the fourth-highest mountain in the world. Flying further, the camera banks just to the east, soars over the not-quite-even-a-village of Dingboche, slings past the Base Camp staging point of Gorakshep, and finally alights on a little foothill called Kala Patthar at the base of the gargantuan Mount Pumori, before turning slowly to the west to look up into the Western Cwm, the main approach to the summit of Everest itself.

Mostly, my fascination with that Google Earth flight simulation was born of simple excitement about the trip. I was ready to go, ready to see these pixelated mountains *for real*, ready to turn the simulation to reality—my faith to sight in a certain sense, I suppose. And so I watched the "flight" over and over again—hundreds of times, I'm sure—changing the angle this time, looking backward that time, pausing and rotating the camera 360 degrees at every point of interest. I showed it to family and friends. I memorized the place-names and the elevations. And over the months that trek route became second nature to me; it was part of me, at the forefront of my mind, so much so that once we actually started the trek, I realized that at any given moment I knew exactly where I was and what was coming up next. I could point to precisely where Mount Everest was relative to my position, even if I couldn't see it at the moment. I knew the Google Earth flyovers were fun; what I didn't realize is that knowing that route so well was preparing me to enjoy the trek even more, precisely because I knew where I was and where I was going.

Some people, of course, might argue that it's better not to know, that part of the joy of a trek like that—or a story or a movie— is relishing each and every surprise. I can certainly respect that. But my own experience is that far from removing the surprise from the trek, knowing what was coming, and knowing what I was seeing at any given moment, *magnified* the beauty of it all. When I saw Mount Ama Dablam emerge from the clouds for the first time, I didn't have to waste time or energy trying to figure out what I was looking at or if it was important. Rather, all the anticipation and excitement of seeing that mountain up close, with my own eyes, immediately shifted into a joyful realization that "This is it! This is Ama Dablam! I've been waiting for this!"

As I've spent the last many years reading the Bible, I've become convinced that having a kind of "Google Earth flyover" of its storyline deeply etched in your mind is an indispensable tool for understanding it rightly—and enjoying the journey. The storyline of the Bible is exquisitely intricate. It's filled with details, backstories, asides, foreshadowing, and flashbacks, and if you're not familiar with its course, you can easily lose sight of what's important—of where you are and where you're going. But knowing the storyline in advance—memorizing the flyover, so to speak—can give you a new and beneficial perspective on the whole experience. So instead of getting lost and confused, you can think things like, "Oh, this is one of the high mountain peaks of the story—the giving of the Law at Sinai." Or, "This next portion will be a long hike, but I know the next important moment will be the crowning of Saul as Israel's first king." You'll know the route, the highest peaks, and the most important vistas of the story. Just as I knew to look forward to Namche and Tengboche and Gorakshep and Kala Patthar, you'll know to be on the lookout for the flood, the crowning of the king, the fall of Jerusalem, and the birth of the Messiah. When you know the landmarks along the trek, they become many things all at once—goals to spur you on, signposts to point you onward to what's coming next, even resting points to take a breath, survey what you've already seen, and look forward to the next leg of the journey.

In this chapter, then, I want to give you a "Google Earth flyover" of the whole storyline of the Bible, from Genesis to Revelation. We won't talk about every detail; I don't want to point out every foothill you're going to encounter or take away every surprise you'll experience. I just want to show you the high mountain peaks. I want you to be able to say at any given point in your reading, "I'm not lost here, not at all. I've just seen [for example] the crowning of the king, and the next big leg of the journey is a long painful slide toward the fall of Jerusalem." In other words, even before we set out on the trek, I want you to have a map in your head.

Years ago, when I was first beginning to study the Bible in depth, a friend recommended I read a short book called *Gospel and Kingdom* by Graeme Goldsworthy. The book was only about sixty pages long as I remember, but its impact on me was worth its weight in gold. I've realized in the years since I read it that Goldsworthy really didn't say anything *new*; that wasn't the value of the book to me.

Its value, rather, was in showing me for the first time that the Bible is not—and is therefore not meant to be *read* as—a collection of unconnected stories or fables. Rather, Goldsworthy taught me that the Bible tells a sweeping story of God's dealings and relationship with human beings, and that that story focuses largely on the history of one particular nation, Israel. I learned so much from that book, but one detail has stuck with me for more than twenty years now— not a particular sentence or paragraph, but a map of Israel's history.[1]

Take a few minutes to study the timeline; memorize it if you can, even if not every detail. I did, over two decades ago, and it has stuck in my mind as the premier guide-map to my reading and understanding of the Bible. At a glance, you can see the main contours of the history of the nation of Israel—the time of the patriarchs, the unified kingdom under David and Solomon, the moment when the nation split into two (Judah in the south, Israel in the north), the exile and demise of the northern kingdom, the exile and eventual return of the southern kingdom, and finally the coming of the Messiah. Along the way, you can see when prophets were proclaiming the word of God, and to which kingdom (north or south) each one mainly preached. No, the map doesn't show everything, but put it in your mind, and it will serve you well on your trek through the biblical story.

The biblical storyline has often been divided into sections, and different Christians have marked those sections in a number of

---

1   The following Outline of Biblical History is taken and adapted from *According to Plan* by Graeme Goldsworthy. Copyright © 1991 by Graeme Goldsworthy. Used by permission of InterVarsity Press, Downers Grove, IL, USA. www.ivpress.com. used by permission of Inter-Varsity Press Limited and reproduced with permission of Inter-Varsity Press Limited through PLSclear.

Outline of Biblical History

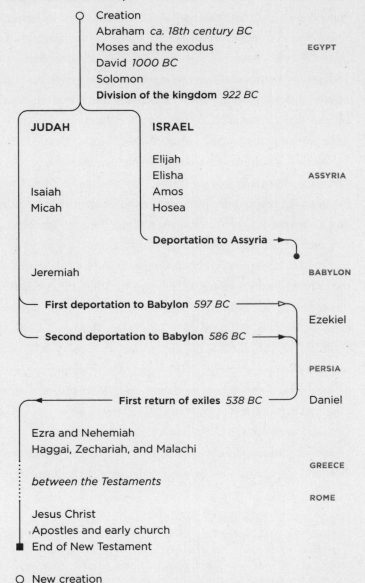

Creation
Abraham *ca. 18th century BC*
Moses and the exodus
David *1000 BC*
Solomon
Division of the kingdom *922 BC*

EGYPT

JUDAH　　　　**ISRAEL**

Elijah
Elisha
Isaiah　　　　Amos
Micah　　　　Hosea

ASSYRIA

Deportation to Assyria

Jeremiah

BABYLON

First deportation to Babylon *597 BC*

Ezekiel

Second deportation to Babylon *586 BC*

PERSIA

First return of exiles *538 BC*　　Daniel

Ezra and Nehemiah
Haggai, Zechariah, and Malachi

GREECE

between the Testaments

ROME

Jesus Christ
Apostles and early church
End of New Testament

O　New creation

different ways. One division of the story that's been proposed, for example, is innocence, conscience, government, promise, law, grace, and kingdom. Another is the simpler (and frankly, I think, more correct and useful) division of creation, fall, redemption, and consummation. What I want to do, though, is not so much divide the story into *sections* as give you a number of high points in the story to be on the lookout for. Moreover, I want to tell you a little about those points—how the story gets to each one and where it heads from there. In the process, I hope you'll become familiar with the narrative's course before you even begin to read it, and that seeing the "pictures" of those high peaks will whet your appetite for the journey ahead. There are ten of them, and you can follow along with Goldsworthy's map.

1. The Creation and the Fall

Every epic story and adventure begins somewhere. A trek to Everest begins at the Lukla airport. The story of Narnia begins in London, and that of the ring in the Shire. The story of the Bible begins where it should in a story like this—at the beginning. The very first words of the Bible, in Genesis 1:1, are: "In the beginning, God created the heavens and the earth." The account of God's creation of the universe unfolds with breakneck speed; there's not much detail given. In fact, of the 1,189 chapters in the Bible, only two of them—Genesis 1 and 2—recount the creation of the universe. Even so, those are critical chapters in the story, for they establish the universal truths that God is sovereign over all the creation, that human beings are accountable to him for how they live, and that right from the very beginning, the creation of human beings was not an accident. Rather, Adam and Eve, the first humans, were created as and to be God's royal image in the world—to rule the world under him and in his name. In other words, they had a job to do.

In the third chapter of the Bible, though—Genesis 3—everything falls apart. This is not by accident, nor due to natural laws, but rather due to Adam and Eve making a decision to rebel against God, his authority, and his crown. Rather than recognizing the limits God placed on them, Adam and Eve decided to listen to the serpent's (that is, Satan's) false promises and eat the fruit that God had forbidden them. That wasn't just a small act of disobedience. It was a declaration of war and independence against God, a determination on their part to join Satan's rebellion against the High King and Creator of the universe, and try to take his throne for themselves.

The results of this were catastrophic. God cursed Satan, the man and the woman, and even the ground itself. Worse, the natural and promised consequence of rebelling against God—death—took hold among human beings. No, Adam and Eve didn't die immediately, but they were cut off from God's presence, cast out of their home in the garden of Eden, and forbidden to return. Through Genesis 4 and 5, death's claws sink deeper and deeper into the human soul, until the drumbeat of Genesis 5 through the generations is only "and he died . . . and he died . . . and he died."

2. The Flood and God's Promises

In the midst of the cataclysm of Genesis 3—right in the middle of the curses God hands down against Adam, Eve, and the serpent—comes a promise that will swell in meaning and intensity through the entire biblical story. Indeed, one could say that this is the promise that animates the whole rest of history. Here's what God says to the serpent in Genesis 3:15:

> I will put enmity between you and the woman,
> and between your offspring and her offspring;
> he shall bruise your head,
> and you shall bruise his heel.

The meaning is at first a bit obscure, but essentially God is promising to send someone else to do what Adam should have done from the moment the serpent tried to conscript Adam into his rebellious war against God. Adam—as God's image, God's vice-regent in the creation—should have then and there crushed the serpent and cast him out of the garden. Instead, he joined the serpent's cause and declared war against God. But here, God declares that against all expectation and hope, all is not lost. One day he will send another man—an offspring of Eve—to finish what Adam failed to do. Satan would die.

One way to look at the Bible's story, therefore, is as the search for an answer to the questions "Who is that offspring? Who will finally defeat the serpent, and how will he do it?" As the story progresses, various characters are held up as potential fulfillments of God's promise. "Is this him?" That's the question that runs through the entire narrative, and one of the first characters who is presented as possibly being the promised offspring is a man named Noah. The events of Noah's life are told in Genesis 6–10. Noah's father initially seems to think that Noah is the fulfillment of the promise of Genesis 3:15 (see Gen. 5:29), and God's salvation of Noah through the universal judgment of the flood seems at first to confirm that.

In a world marked by rank wickedness and sin, maybe it's this man—Noah the righteous one—who will set everything right.

The Bible's description of the worldwide flood is incredibly dramatic, and its point is that the sin unleashed in Genesis 3 by Adam's rebellion has finally filled the world to the brim. The wickedness of men cries out for judgment and destruction, and so God wipes out humankind. There's still hope, though! Righteous Noah and his family are closed up by God's kindness in the ark (a Hebrew word that means simply "box," but obviously refers here to a boat) and are kept safe through the flood. After several months, when the doors open and the rainbow shines down, it looks like Genesis 3:15 has come to pass. The wicked are dead, sin is no more, and righteous Noah can start over.

Or so it seemed. Tragically, at the end of Genesis 9 it becomes clear that all is not well after all. Noah sins in his drunkenness, his sons sin in their mockery of their father, and Noah's life ends with the same iron refrain that marked Genesis 5: "and he died" (9:29). Indeed, by the end of Genesis 11, it's clear that sin has not been eradicated from the human race, even by the pruning of it back to *the most righteous* man of all. Rather, the people of the earth join together in their pride to build a tower to the heavens, intending once again to rival God himself—a project God frustrates by scrambling the languages of men. Chapter 11 ends with this brutal truth about a man named Terah, an idol-worshiper from a city called Ur: "and Terah died."

3. The Exodus

Starting in Genesis 12, the pace of the biblical story slows considerably. For the next thirty-eight chapters, through the rest of the book, Genesis tells the story of the patriarchs of the nation of Israel. God first calls Abraham, the son of Terah, and makes a set of spectacular promises to him: not only will God make a great nation of Abraham and give him a land in which to live, but also *all* the nations of the earth will be blessed through one of his offspring. The resonance is unmistakable: the promised offspring of Genesis 3:15 will be a descendant of this man.

Abraham eventually has two sons, Ishmael and Isaac, and his faith is sorely and wonderfully tested through the years of his life. Will Abraham trust God to keep his promises, or he will lose faith and turn away from following God? That's the question he faces over and over through his 175 years. Ultimately, Abraham dies, and God reiterates the promises to his son Isaac, and then again to Isaac's son Jacob. In each generation, the details of the events may be different, but the question is the same: Will you trust God to keep his promises? And each man, imperfectly but truly, ultimately answers yes. Around chapter 35, the story of Genesis takes an unexpected turn. Until now, the line of the promises had been remarkably straight—from Abraham to Isaac to Jacob. Now, though, Jacob has twelve sons, and for the rest of the book, it's not clear to which of those sons the promises are going to fall. The first-, second-, and third-born all disqualify themselves in particular ways, and it seems that the fourth-born, Judah, does the same. Then for fourteen chapters, it looks as if the promises are destined to fall to Jacob's next-to-youngest, a boy named Joseph whom God raises to royalty in the empire of Egypt. In fact, by the end of Genesis the reader's heart is meant to be swelling with hope; maybe, just maybe, this Joseph is the promised one who would set everything right.

The beginning of the book of Exodus, however, lays those hopes to a rough rest. "Then Joseph died," it begins, "and all his brothers and all that generation. . . . Now there arose a new king over Egypt, who did not know Joseph" (Ex. 1:6, 8). Despite all the promise, despite the dizzying height to which Joseph had risen, this new king crushes the people of Israel under his foot, subjecting them to grinding slavery. But once again, hope is not lost. As the people cried out, Exodus tells us in smoldering language: "God heard their groaning, and God remembered his covenant with Abraham, with Isaac, and with Jacob. God saw the people of Israel—and God knew" (Ex. 2:24–25).

The word *exodus* means, simply, "exit." God's freeing of his people from slavery in Egypt is the third towering mountain peak in the epic story of the Bible. The events are recounted in Exodus 1–20: how God miraculously saved the life of a baby named Moses, then called him to confront Pharaoh; how God waged war against the false gods of Egypt and essentially de-created that nation from the bottom up; how he saved his people from death by teaching them about the reality and meaning of a substitutionary sacrifice—a lamb slain and its blood put on their doorposts so that they and their children would not have to die.

The exodus of the people of Israel from Egypt is, without doubt, the most important event in the entire Old Testament. The psalmists, the prophets, the kings, the scribes—all of them will look back time and time again to the moment when their God broke an empire in order to save them, to redeem them from slavery. Why was the exodus so important? It wasn't just that the people were saved from a horrific circumstance, though that would have been great enough in itself. It was that the people of Israel learned, more clearly than they had yet seen, about the unassailable power of their God, about his universal sovereignty, and about *how* he intended to save his people once and for all in the future. Indeed the exodus became—even up to and through the New Testament—a kind of paradigm of God's saving work. "This is how he does it" is the message, and by studying it, we see how God will save his people once and for all in the end—without their help, by his grace, and through atoning sacrifice.

4. The Conquest

Having rescued his people from Egypt, God leads them to Mount Sinai, where he establishes a covenant with them—they are to be his people and he is to be their God. The rest of the book of Exodus, and subsequently Leviticus, Numbers, and Deuteronomy, recount Israel's halting and finally tragic approach to the land God had promised to give Abraham. Those books are full of drama, intrigue, and action, but they are also full of the laws God gave to his people, laws that taught both God's own holiness and righteousness *and* the responsibility of the people to obey him, follow him, and worship him only. The book of Deuteronomy records Moses's last words to the people before his death, as they're camped on the banks of the Jordan River, the last obstacle between them and the Promised Land. That's a poignant moment, because the first time the Israelites had been on the border of the land, they'd rebelled against God again, refusing to trust him and instead giving themselves over to fear and unbelief in God's promises; thus God had left them to wander in the desert until an entire generation of them died. Now, it was a new generation camping on the banks of the Jordan, but the question facing them was the same one that faced their parents at a different time and different place: Would they trust God to keep his promises or not?

The book of Deuteronomy ends with the great leader Moses's death, and the book of Joshua picks up immediately with the recounting of the conquest of Canaan. This was the land God had promised to Abraham, and now, with a man named Joshua at their head, the people of Israel sweep through the land, delivering God's justice against the wicked, child-sacrificing peoples who inhabited it and receiving what God had promised to them. The Jordan River dries up, the walls of Jericho fall *outward* (as if an enormous bomb were detonated in the center of the city), Israel's enemies are routed, and Canaan's cities fall into Israel's hands. Again and again, the lesson is the same: if the people and their leaders will trust in God and obey him, the fruits of the land will be theirs; if not, they'll know only disaster and defeat.

By the end of the book of Joshua, the conquest seems all but finished, and Joshua begins the work of dividing up the land among the descendants of the twelve sons of Jacob—that is, the twelve tribes of Israel. The book, though, ends with perhaps a small storm cloud on the horizon, saying that "Israel served the LORD all the days of Joshua, and all the days of the elders who outlived Joshua and had known all the work that the LORD did for Israel." Of course, that's great, but it's hardly "happily ever after." What would happen once all those who had seen everything God had done for Israel were gone?

The book of Judges tells us, and it's not pretty. Often Christians will read the book of Judges as if it's a simple collection

of short stories, fables that teach one lesson or another about faith in God. But Judges is actually doing far more than that; it's pushing the story forward, especially in proving that Israel desperately needs a king. The pattern of Judges is well known: Israel fails to do what God commands and finds herself under the foot of one or another oppressor nation. They pray to God, who raises up a "judge" (meaning a military leader) to save them, and once freed from oppression, Israel quickly spirals back down into faithlessness and idolatry. What finally becomes clear is that Judges is tracing a stomach-turning, spiraling plummet of the nation into paganism, chaos, and wickedness—so much so that the final chapters of the book recount a maelstrom of murder, pagan human sacrifice, and idolatry (even by Moses's own grandson!). The books ends with a refrain that sounds several times through the book, part accusation, part lament, part prayer: "In those days there was no king in Israel. Everyone did what was right in his own eyes" (Judg. 21:25).

5. The Crown

The next high peak in the Bible's story comes in the books of Samuel, with the crowning of the first king of Israel and the eventual, long-awaited coronation of the famous King David. It's a glorious moment not only in Israel's history as a nation coming into its own, but also because as the crown is placed on the king's head, the promise of Genesis 3:15 still pulses in the background: Maybe this is the one. Maybe this king will succeed where King Adam failed.

Before the mountain peaks of Samuel, though, comes the idyllic, almost comically out-of-place book of Ruth. The book tells of

a woman named Ruth who, after the death of her husband and father-in-law, accompanies her mother-in-law, Naomi, back to her hometown, a village called Bethlehem in the heart of the Promised Land. When they arrive, it turns out that neither Ruth nor Naomi has the means to support themselves, so Naomi hatches a plot to have Ruth brought under the care of a distant relative named Boaz. The story progresses with humor and surprise, and through most of it the reader is left amused but wondering why this book is here in the first place. The answer comes at the end. Boaz and Ruth skid through one last obstacle and get married, and the book ends with the happy news: "A son has been born to Naomi." (Actually, he was born to Ruth and Boaz, but the child saves Naomi's family line from extinction, so the blessing is hers as well.) And then the punchline, with a knowing smile: "They named him Obed. He was the father of Jesse, the father of David" (Ruth 4:17).

The name David, right there at the end of this charming love story, lands like a thunderclap. It turns out this book wasn't just an out-of-place romantic comedy after all, but a bridge to the crown. It would be some time before David would be crowned king once and for all, but already the plot is straining forward in that happy direction.

The two books of Samuel tell how kingship came to Israel. At first Israel is ruled by a man who seems, at once, to be the nation's last judge and the first prophet—Samuel. He rules faithfully but imperfectly, and eventually the people demand that Samuel anoint a king over them, one who would rule "like all the nations" (1 Sam. 8:5). Samuel objects to the request, but the problem isn't in the people's desire for a king; God had told them

many times already that he would eventually give them a king, Judges had cried out for one, and Ruth smiled at the prospect. No, the problem was that they wanted a king who would not be the kind of king God wanted, but a king "like all the nations." They did not ask for a king who would lead the nation to trust God for security and salvation, but who would promise such safety and well-being *by his own power*. So, God gave them what they wanted: a king tall, strong, and handsome, a king like all the nations—Saul.

And, just as God knew and Samuel promised, this was a disaster. Most of 1 Samuel tells the story of Saul's slow demise, of his own insecurity and pride growing until it consumed him. Ultimately, he not only disobeyed God in high-handed rebellion but even sought out a necromancer—one who by witchcraft sought to speak to the dead—in a desperate bid to hang on to his crown. The account of Saul ends with the metaphorical statement about him and his men: "Then they rose and went away that night" (1 Sam. 28:25). The sun of Saul the king had finally set.

Poignantly, the next chapter of 1 Samuel tells us this: "So David set out with his men early in the morning" (1 Sam. 29:11). Saul's sun was sinking below the horizon, but David's morning was finally breaking. It had been a long time coming. God had actually commanded Samuel to anoint David as the next king way back in chapter 16, but it's not until after Saul's death and a struggle for the crown that all the tribes of Israel finally come to David in 2 Samuel 5 to declare him king of a united Israel. From there, David conquers the city of Jerusalem, makes it his royal capital, and joyfully brings the ark of the covenant into its walls. David's reign is recognized as a golden age in Israel's history, eclipsed only by that of his son Solomon. The nation is united, its enemies are defeated, and the worship of the one true God is regulated and centralized in the Royal City of Jerusalem. Finally, there is a king in Israel.

6. The Exile

Even so, all was not well. For all his glory and victories, even for being "a man after [God's] own heart" (1 Sam. 13:14), David, it turns out, is not the great promised offspring of Genesis 3:15. In the book of 2 Samuel, he commits adultery and murder, and his family eventually dissolves into civil war. His son Solomon isn't the promised one either. Though God had given him wealth and wisdom beyond imagining, Solomon sins against God as well, ultimately becoming exactly the kind of self-interested king Samuel had warned about. When Solomon dies, the kingdom falls to his son Rehoboam, whose foolishness and cruelty result in the breaking of the kingdom into two separate nations, two separate crowns, two separate histories.

The books of Kings and Chronicles record the activities of the various kings of these two nations—the nation of Israel in the north, and the nation of Judah in the south. With few exceptions, the history of both nations' kings echo that of the book of Judges—a stomach-turning descent into wickedness, paganism, and idolatry. In the midst of this descent, however, God begins to send men to call the people of Israel and Judah to repentance and back to faithfulness to him. This is the age of the prophets. The books of 1 and 2 Kings focus most of their attention on two prophets in particular, Elijah and his successor Elisha, but there were others as well, which you can see in Goldsworthy's map. Most of the twelve Minor Prophets—the last twelve books of the Old Testament—prophesied during this period of the kings, either in the north or the south. Rather than reading the Minor Prophets all at once at the end of the Old Testament, it's more beneficial and enlightening to read them at the point in the story of Kings when they were actually prophesying.[2]

Ultimately, the wickedness of both Israel and Judah—and their kings—constituted a permanent breach of God's covenant with them, and in 721 BC the king of Assyria invaded the northern kingdom of Israel. Its cities were destroyed, its people were carried away into exile, and ten of the twelve tribes of Israel were dissolved into the nations and never heard from again. God spared the southern kingdom for about another century, but then in 586 BC the empire of Babylon invaded. Jerusalem was destroyed, and the people of the kingdom of Judah were carried away into exile just like their northern brethren.

It's probably not exactly right to call the exile a "high peak" of the biblical storyline. It's really far more like a dark and foreboding valley, but no less notable because of that. For the people of Israel, the exile was a cataclysm, a political *and theological* disaster. How could this happen? How could God abandon his covenant people Israel, his city Jerusalem, his covenant king, David? Had God failed to keep his promises, even to Abraham? What about Genesis 3:15? If there's no king and no dynasty,

---

2 I recommend the suggested reading plan found at https://www.crossway.org/books/the-epic-story-of-the-bible-tpb/. This plan tells you exactly when to read each of the Minor Prophets, leads you through them with commentary, and then takes you right back to where you left off in the story of the kings.

how can there ever be the promised one to crush the head of the serpent?

7. The Return

Even before the last hammer blows of the exile fell, before King Nebuchadnezzar of Babylon invaded—even before Babylon rose to the power of an empire—God began promising his people that their exile would not be their end. That's the story that lies behind the books of the four Major Prophets—Isaiah, Jeremiah, Ezekiel, and Daniel. Those four books were written at different times, in different places, and from different perspectives, but together they form a kind of four-part harmony of God's promises to save his people from exile. Isaiah prophesied about 150 years before the fall of Jerusalem, and his book is a beautiful prophecy of judgment for sin being exhausted and ended in one who is identified as, variously, the King, the servant, and the conqueror.[3] Jeremiah, for his part, lived through the fall of Jerusalem itself, and his prophecies reflected the chaotic nature of the invasion but held forth God's promise to forge a new covenant with his people from the broken shards of the old one. Different from both Isaiah and Jeremiah, Ezekiel was among those who were carried away from Jerusalem to exile in Babylon; his prophecies not only wrestled with *why* God had executed this judgment, but also looked forward to the day when the people of Israel would return to their land and rebuild the capital city of Jerusalem.

Finally that happened, in 536 BC. In that year Cyrus the Persian, having taken the city of Babylon in a sneak attack, decreed that the Jews could return to their homeland and rebuild their

---

3   J. Alec Motyer, *The Prophecy of Isaiah: An Introduction and Commentary* (Downers Grove, IL: IVP Academic, 1993), 13–16.

city and its temple. The story of that return is told in the books of Ezra and Nehemiah, but it turns out not to be the glorious, sun-bathed mountain peak that you might expect. Yes, the people manage—through many obstacles and much opposition—to rebuild Jerusalem's walls and even its temple. But something was wrong. Despite the prayers of the people, despite their hopes that God would fill the temple with his presence just as he had at the dedication of Solomon's temple . . . nothing happened this time. As Ezra put it, "Many of the priests and Levites and heads of fathers' houses, old men who had seen the first house, wept with a loud voice when they saw the foundation of this house being laid" (Ezra 3:12), because its glory could not compare.

The Old Testament thus ends on a decidedly mixed note—joy because the people of Israel are back in their land, yet sorrow because the covenant is broken and unrepairable. The last prophet of the Old Testament, Malachi, captured both those emotions in his prophecy, castigating the people for robbing God and committing adultery against him, and yet renewing the promise—yet again—that one would come who would finally purify their sins in a refiner's fire.

Then, for 435 years, God said nothing.

8. The Messiah

The New Testament opens with the declaration that the long awaited promised one—the offspring of Genesis 3:15, the promised King, the Messiah—has finally arrived. The word *Messiah* is a Hebrew word that means simply "anointed one" (translated into Greek, it's "Christ"), which could refer to kings, priests, or any other officials who were specially anointed with oil as a way of consecrating them to their duties. Over time, though, it took on the specialized meaning of *the* anointed one, referring to the one who would finally and fully fulfill all the promises of salvation and redemption that God had made in the Old Testament.

All four of the gospels—Matthew, Mark, Luke, and John—declare that those promises had finally been fulfilled by a man named Jesus, born in Bethlehem and raised in Nazareth. Descended from David, he claims the fallen crown of Israel as his own and, infinitely more, he proclaims that he is God-become-man. No longer would God merely rule his people *through* a king; now he would rule his people *as* king. Again and again, Jesus performs miracles that not only show his boundless power but also reveal that he himself is the fulfillment of all the foreshadowings, all the signs, all the symbols and themes of the Old Testament. It all comes to rest on him.

Even so, the Jewish people reject him, and Jesus declares that his kingship, his salvation, his offer of mercy is no longer for them alone but rather now—just as the Old Testament had foretold— for *anyone* from any nation who would bow the knee to him and trust in him for salvation. Not all the Jews rejected Jesus, of course. But as a whole, the nation decides that this man can't possibly be the king they've been waiting for. He's not a military leader; he has no ambitions of overthrowing the Roman Empire; he is poor and unimpressive. And yet, for all that, the Jewish leaders realize that he is a threat to their status and their position. So they plot with the Romans, pay one of his disciples to betray him, and condemn him to die by crucifixion.

What they didn't realize, however, was that this too, even his death, was a fulfillment of prophecy, and the explosive, breathtaking climax of God's plan of redemption. Why? Because God had promised all along that humanity's sin could be forgiven and paid for only by penalty of death—either the death of the sinner himself or the death of a substitutionary sacrifice in the sinner's place. And ultimately, he had prophesied that it would be the Messiah, God-made-man, who would himself *be* that sacrifice. So the Messiah died that day, and the Old Testament was once and for all fulfilled . . .

. . . except for one more thing. See, the Old Testament had also prophesied that God would not leave the Messiah to rot in the grave, but rather that he would set him on high to rule forever as King of kings and Lord of lords. So on the third day after his death, Jesus the Messiah rose from the dead. Over the next forty days, he appeared numerous times to his disciples, teaching them, caring for them, strengthening them, preparing them. He taught them the good news of salvation through trust in him, and he commissioned them to proclaim that good news—that "gospel"—to all the nations of the world.

9. The Church

Beginning with the book of Acts, then, the New Testament recounts the history of the first few decades of Jesus's people in the wake of his resurrection and ascension. In Matthew 16, Jesus had organized and established his people into what he called the *church*, a word that means simply "the assembly," but which Jesus described not just as a mob but as something more like a royal embassy. These churches, he said, would herald his message of royal grace, calling people around the world to trust in Jesus, bow to him as King, and receive mercy from his hand. They would speak for him, defending the truth of the gospel and declaring with his authority who has rightly embraced it. In short, as he told his people just before his ascension, they would be his witnesses in Jerusalem, Judea, Samaria, and the uttermost parts of the earth (Acts 1:8).

The book of Acts records the early spread of the gospel of Jesus through the region. About halfway through, its focus lights on a man named Saul, whom Jesus himself confronts on the road as he is on his way to persecute Christians in the city of Damascus. Saul—whom Jesus renamed as Paul—is utterly convinced of Jesus's resurrection and the reality of his saving kingship, and he becomes a veritable juggernaut of missionary activity, spreading the gospel and planting new churches—new embassies of the King—throughout the Roman Empire. In the process, Paul also became the church's foremost theologian and pastor, writing thirteen letters to the various churches he'd planted (four of which—1 and 2 Timothy, Titus, and Philemon—were more personal in nature, but were still deemed to be of general benefit to the church), in which he taught and defended the gospel, corrected error, and encouraged Christians to remain firm in the faith. Like the Minor Prophets in the Old Testament, the letters of Paul are collected in one place in the New Testament, and not in any particularly logical order (in fact, believe it or not, they're ordered roughly from longest to shortest!). So the best way to read them is to pause your reading of Acts and read each one when it was written; what emerges is a vibrant and action-filled story in which Paul struggles to ensure that the churches don't finally reject the faith altogether.[4] Taken together, Paul's and the other apostles' letters are a deeply encour-

4 Just as for the Minor Prophets, the suggested reading plan found at https://www. crossway.org/books/the-epic-story-of-the-bible-tpb/ tells you exactly when to read each of Paul's and the other apostles' letters, leads you through each one with commentary, and then takes you right back to where you left off in the story of Acts.

aging and long-abiding source of comfort to Jesus's people, even as we wait on his promised return.

10. The End

The Bible ends with the Revelation to the apostle John, given to him while he was in exile on the prison-isle of Patmos. Condemned to die there for his stubborn preaching of the gospel of Jesus in the face of official demands to stop, John was shown a series of visions by God which were meant to encourage him, and the rest of the beleaguered church, with the reminder that no matter what they might suffer, their King Jesus is still on the throne, and in the end he wins. Revelation is a trip of a book, filled with astonishing images, sometimes bewildering symbolism, and cosmic visions that reveal a reality that goes far beyond what our eyes can see. The details are fascinating, important, and astounding, but the main point of the book is bracing and spine-steeling: Yes, Jesus's people will suffer; yes, Satan will rage against them, and in so many ways he will seem to have triumphed. But King Jesus will return one day. With salvation for his people and vengeance for those who crushed them, he will return and establish his kingdom forever and ever.

That's how the Bible ends—with God's people gathered into the new Jerusalem, even a new Eden—never to be threatened by sin again, never to be separated from God's presence again. Jesus the King protects them, keeps them, heals them, and sustains them, and at the highest peak of all, the very Everest of the entire Bible, we find this joyous promise:

> Then the angel showed me the river of the water of life, bright as crystal, flowing from the throne of God and of the Lamb

through the middle of the street of the city; also, on either side of the river, the tree of life with its twelve kinds of fruit, yielding its fruit each month. The leaves of the tree were for the healing of the nations. No longer will there be anything accursed, but the throne of God and of the Lamb will be in it, and his servants will worship him. They will see his face, and his name will be on their foreheads. And night will be no more. They will need no light of lamp or sun, for the Lord God will be their light, and they will reign forever and ever. (Rev. 22:1–5)

At the end of a world in which humans were cast away from God, and flaming swords of angels barred their way to the tree of life, and a thick curtain separated them from his presence, these words—"they will see his face"—are breathtakingly beautiful. Because of what Jesus the Messiah has done, it is, finally, finished.

Conclusion

If you've never read the Bible—or maybe even if you have!—I realize that's a lot of information. Maybe you've even read the Bible a dozen times in your life but never realized that the story it tells is quite so linear and well-defined. Maybe you're daunted by the thought of diving into a story that seems so intricate and detailed. I get it. And believe me, the story is far deeper and more sophisticated than what I've given you here. These are just the high points. But there's still something useful in knowing where you're going. If you're setting out to read the 1,178 pages of Tolkien's *The Lord of the Rings*, it's helpful to know that your signposts are something like "First the Shire, then Rivendell, then the Mines of Moria, then Rohan and Helm's Deep and Mordor, and finally Gondor." If you're going to Everest, it's "First Lukla, then Namche, then Tengboche and Dingboche and Gorakshep, and finally Base Camp." Yes, it's a rough map to hold in your mind, but on a journey like that, any map is helpful!

Likewise, I hope these "high peaks" of the biblical storyline will provide a kind of stability and comfort and even encouragement as you read: First the creation, then the flood, then the exodus and the conquest and the crown. Next comes the exile and return, then the Messiah, the church, and finally the end. Sure, there will be some long, hard hikes between the peaks; you may even need to come back to this chapter again to get your bearings. But at least you'll be able to see them, the high peaks shining in the light, and that in itself will help you press on to the next one.

3

My Dwelling Place

The Theme of God's Presence

IN THE LOWER ELEVATIONS of the Himalayas, if you time it just right, you can see the mountains explode with color as the forests of rhododendron trees bloom in a fireworks display of white, pink, and bright red flowers. This surprised me. My impression of the Himalayas, before I arrived, was mainly formed by what I'd seen in movies and internet pictures—the craggy, snow-capped mountains you're probably thinking of, too. To be sure, the trees eventually give way to that kind of barren, but still beautiful in its own way, moonscape; but until you get above about five thousand meters elevation, the Himalayas look more like a lush forest than anything else.

And my goodness, the flowers! Standing on a ridge overlooking the Khumbu Valley, you can see the mountain faces on both sides of the glacier river below alive with forests of rhododendrons. I'd seen blooming forests before. Some of the pine forests where I grew up in East Texas were also dotted with dogwood trees, which would bloom in the spring. On certain days when the blooms were past their prime and the wind was high, you could walk through the forest and imagine you were in a fairy tale—white dogwood petals fluttering down around you in a magic rainfall as far as the eye could see. That was beautiful, but it was nothing like what I saw in the Himalayas. Patches and swirls of red, pink, and white swept across every mountainside, giving way only every so often to streaks of green—some light, some darker—that rolled down to meet the ice-blue water of the glacier river in the valley below. And towering above it all, in the distance, were the snowcaps, the majestic and fearsome peaks that rule the Himalayas from high above.

Many years ago, a friend of mine used an illustration about reading the Bible that reminded me of those rhododendron forests with their different-colored flowers. He was explaining the difference between what Christian scholars call "systematic theology" and what they call "biblical theology." Maybe you've never heard those terms; maybe they don't even sound all that different to you. I mean, we want our theology to be both systematic *and* biblical, right? But that's not exactly what those terms are getting at. Imagine you are walking through a forest, and you notice that the environment around you is filled with different-colored flowers—purple violets, white daisies, yellow daffodils, red roses (do forests have roses? I don't know; it doesn't matter; just stick with me here). Now imagine that you want to study all the flowers in that forest. One way to do that would be to gather up each kind of flower and look at them in a bunch—all the roses, all the daffodils, etc.—to see what you can learn about each kind of flower.

That's what *systematic theology* does with the teachings of the Bible; roughly speaking, it tries to grasp and understand everything the entire Bible teaches about certain topics like God, salvation, Jesus, the church, and others. *Biblical theology* is somewhat different. Its main approach is not to gather the flowers up, but rather to study them where they appear in the forest. So instead of saying, "Oh, look how all these roses are shaped in a certain way; they all seem to share this in common," biblical theology says, "Oh, look how those roses sit next to those daisies, how they interact with them. And look! There's another rose bush over there, and there, too! And look how they sweep up the side of that mountain, too." In other words, biblical theology tries to see how different truths *sit* and *develop* as the storyline of the Bible unfolds.

Obviously there are benefits to both of these ways of studying the Bible, and neither is ever completely independent of the other. Systematic theology helps us to understand what the Bible as a whole teaches about various truths, but without forgetting that the Bible is, after all, a story; biblical theology helps us see how those truths develop and unfold through the narrative as God reveals more and more truth about them, but without forgetting that the Bible, after all, will never contradict itself. Both are useful; each is governed by the other. For the most part, though, the journey we're about to set off on here—to read the Bible straight through as one epic story—is an exercise mostly in *biblical theology*. We're going to see how the doctrines and themes that structure and color the Bible develop and grow as the narrative progresses, and ultimately how they come to fulfillment in the New Testament.

In the next few chapters, therefore, I'll introduce you to some of the main themes you're going to encounter as you read the Bible, and give you an overview of how each one develops throughout the course of the narrative. Similar to the narrative flyover of the last chapter, I won't tell you everything about these themes; there will still be surprises as you read! But it will help to have an idea ahead of time about where each one of them goes, how they twist and turn and develop and bank around corners, and ultimately where each of them lands. That kind of advance knowledge will help you read the Bible with more confidence and, ultimately, more enjoyment. In all honesty, there are far more theological and narrative themes in the Bible than we have time to consider here. As you read, you'll probably identify many others that I don't even mention; but that's good. That kind of discovery is part of the fun! For now, I want to introduce you to four of the Bible's main themes, which weave in and around each other to shape the main course of the biblical epic. Those themes are God's presence, covenant, the kingship, and sacrifice. Let's start with the theme of God's presence.

———

The presence of God with his people is one of the most prominent themes in the entire Bible, running from the very first chapters of Genesis to the very last chapters of Revelation, and even arguably giving shape to the central riddle of the entire storyline: How can a perfectly righteous and holy God ever have rebellious, sinful human beings in his presence without destroying them in his righteous wrath? In the Jewish mind, God's presence was tied inextricably to the temple in Jerusalem. And no wonder! God had made it clear that he intended to dwell among his people, and he'd commissioned King Solomon (David's son) to build the temple and then dramatically filled it with his presence on the day it was consecrated. That was a glorious moment, one that lived in the Jewish mind for centuries. But it was a long time in the making—going back, in fact, all the way to Adam and Eve in the garden of Eden.

Presence in the Garden

After the creation of Adam and Eve, the first human beings, the Bible makes it clear that they lived in the garden of Eden in the full enjoyment of the presence of God. The picture of God's relationship with Adam is of a wonderful, fatherly intimacy right from the moment of creation. God "breathed into his nostrils the breath of life," he lovingly "planted a garden in Eden, in the east, and there he put the man whom he had formed. And out of the ground the Lord God made to spring up every tree that is pleasant to the sight and good for food" (Gen. 2:7–9). Genesis 3:8 even implies that it was a normal and frequent thing for God to "walk in the garden in the cool of the day" with Adam and Eve—they and he in perfect, unbroken fellowship and harmony.

Interestingly, the very nature of the garden of Eden, and what God intended Adam to do in it, points to the fellowship he and Adam enjoyed together. In Genesis 2:15, God places Adam in the garden and tells him that he is to "work it and keep it." At first, those words look pretty unremarkable; after all, working and keeping a garden seem like perfectly natural things to do. But there's more going on there than meets the eye. The word "work" is the Hebrew word *abad*, and it points to the fact that Adam was to be the caretaker of the garden, to cultivate it and encourage its growth in maturity and beauty. The word "keep," though, is not just a synonym for "work." It's the Hebrew word *shamar,* and it means much more than just keeping the garden presentable. What it means is that Adam was to guard the garden and protect it, making sure that nothing evil or unclean ever entered it, and if it did, to make sure that evil was judged and cast out. We'll talk about that more in chapter 5, but here's the kicker: These two words—*abad* ("work") and *shamar* ("keep")—are the precise job description given not only to Adam but also eventually to the priests in Israel's temple (which started out as a tent, or "tabernacle"). So when God first tells Moses to give the priests their instructions, he says of them, "They shall *guard* [*shamar*] all the furnishings of the tent of meeting, and keep *guard* [*shamar*] over the people of Israel as they *minister* [*abad*] at the tabernacle" (Num. 3:8). Then, when God describes to Aaron the duties of the priests (Num. 18:1–7), the two words show up over and over as they are told to do the ministry [*abad*] of the tabernacle and keep guard [*shamar*] over it. You see the point? The garden of Eden was, in its very essence, a perfect temple.[1] It was the dwelling place of God with man, the place where man and God met, the place where they walked together in the cool of the day. And like the priests who would *abad* and *shamar* the tabernacle and the temple, so Adam was to *abad* and *shamar* the *original* temple of the garden of Eden.

Of course, Adam failed catastrophically at that task. Instead of fulfilling his duty as the priestly "keeper" of God's temple—judg-

---

1   See G. K. Beale, *The Temple and the Church's Mission: A Biblical Theology of the Dwelling Place of God,* NSBT (Downers Grove, IL: InterVarsity, 2004) and T. D. Alexander, *From Eden to the New Jerusalem: An Introduction to Biblical Theology* (Grand Rapids, MI: Kregel Academic & Professional, 2009).

ing the serpent and casting it out of the garden—Adam abdicated his responsibility and allowed sin to enter. The result was that Adam and Eve's sin broke their fellowship with God and placed them outside his presence. The second part of Genesis 3:8 puts it succinctly. As God was calling for them in the cool of the day, "the man and his wife hid themselves from the presence of the LORD God among the trees of the garden." It's interesting that it's Adam and Eve themselves who do the hiding. Sin does that; it makes people want to flee from the presence of the Lord. But the breaking of fellowship between these first humans and God wasn't just a matter of them hiding. Their sin had objectively separated them from God's presence already, a fact underscored when God casts them out of the garden-temple altogether and bolts the door against them:

> Therefore the LORD God sent him out from the garden of Eden to work the ground from which he was taken. He drove out the man, and at the east of the garden of Eden he placed the cherubim and a flaming sword that turned every way to guard the way to the tree of life. (Gen. 3:23–24)

Provisional Presence

It's not inaccurate to say that the rest of the Bible is the story of God moving heaven and earth to bring human beings back into his presence, to deal with sin once and for all so they could be invited—holy and righteous and justified—back into his presence with joy. Indeed there are glimpses of God's intent to do this very thing throughout the first few books of the Bible. When God confirms his promises to Abraham in Genesis 17, he tells him that the goal of it all is "to be God to you and to your offspring after you" (v. 7). In other words, God intends, yet again, to be in relationship with human beings rather than separated from them. The story of Jacob having a vision of a ladder stretching from heaven to earth, with angels ascending and descending on it, seems to have a similar message: God's promise is to one day bridge the yawning gap between heaven and earth that had been opened by human sin. In Exodus, too, even before God rescues Israel from slavery, he takes a personal interest in them, saying to Pharaoh: "Thus says the LORD, Israel is my firstborn son, and I say to you, 'Let my son go that he may serve me'" (Ex. 4:22–23). A few chapters later, he puts the matter even more sharply:

> Say therefore to the people of Israel, "I am the LORD, and I will bring you out from under the burdens of the Egyptians, and I will deliver you from slavery to them, and I will redeem you with an outstretched arm and with great acts of judgment. I will take you to be my people, and I will be your God, and you shall know that I am the LORD your God, who has brought you out from under the burdens of the Egyptians." (Ex. 6:6–7)

At least in a provisional sort of way, the separation between God and humans would be ended, and he would dwell among them as their God once more.

But God's presence among the people was only provisional, and it was enormously dangerous. The first glimpse we see of this in the Bible's story comes immediately after God rescues the people from Egypt. In Exodus 19, the people have made their way to the foot of a mountain just outside Egypt called Mount Sinai. It's a pivotal moment in the story because this is when God puts himself into covenant with Israel, taking them as his own people. As Israel gathers around the mountain, the theme of God's presence is unmistakable; he is about to descend from heaven to be with them.

> On the third new moon after the people of Israel had gone out of the land of Egypt, on that day they came into the wilderness of Sinai. They set out from Rephidim and came into the wilderness of Sinai, and they encamped in the wilderness. There Israel encamped before the mountain, while Moses went up to God. The LORD called to him out of the mountain, saying, "Thus you shall say to the house of Jacob, and tell the people of Israel: 'You yourselves have seen what I did to the Egyptians, and how I bore you on eagles' wings and brought you to myself. Now therefore, if you will indeed obey my voice and keep my covenant, you shall be my treasured possession among all peoples, for all the earth is mine; and you shall be to me a kingdom of priests and a holy nation.' These are the words that you shall speak to the people of Israel."
>
> So Moses came and called the elders of the people and set before them all these words that the LORD had commanded him. All the people answered together and said, "All that the LORD has spoken we will do." And Moses reported the words of the people to the LORD. And the LORD said to Moses, "Behold, I am coming to you in a thick cloud, that the people may hear when I speak with you, and may also believe you forever." (Ex. 19:1–9)

Do you see what's happening here? God reminds the people of what he's done for them in saving them from slavery, and he tells them what is required of them now. Then they, in turn, agree to do those things so that they can enjoy all the benefits of being his singularly treasured possession. But the greatest benefit comes in verse 9: "I am coming to you." God is about to make himself *present* once again among human beings.

All is not easy and relaxed, though. Look at what God tells Moses to do in preparation for his coming:

> The LORD said to Moses, "Go to the people and consecrate them today and tomorrow, and let them wash their garments and be ready for the third day. For on the third day the LORD will come down on Mount Sinai in the sight of all the people. And you shall set limits for the people all around, saying, 'Take care not to go up into the mountain or touch the edge of it. Whoever touches the mountain shall be put to death. No hand shall touch him, but he shall be stoned or shot; whether beast or man, he shall not live.'" . . .
>
> On the morning of the third day there were thunders and lightnings and a thick cloud on the mountain and a very loud trumpet blast, so that all the people in the camp trembled. Then Moses brought the people out of the camp to meet God, and they took their stand at the foot of the mountain. Now Mount Sinai was wrapped in smoke because the LORD had descended on it in fire. The smoke of it went up like the smoke of a kiln, and the whole mountain trembled greatly. And as the sound of the trumpet grew louder and louder, Moses spoke, and God answered him in thunder. (Ex. 19:10–19)

So God takes the people of Israel as his own—they will be his people, and he will be their God—and he will even be present among them. But there are limits. Yes, Israel is invited once again into the presence of God, but it's not like it was in Eden. There will be no leisurely walks through the garden in the cool of the day, no easy-like-Sunday-morning conversation between God and man. This was an invitation, but not an open one. In fact, as you can see in the verses above, the people of Israel wouldn't even be allowed to come up the mountain to see God. Their access to God would be only through a mediator of God's own choice: "The LORD came down on Mount Sinai, to the top of the mountain. And the LORD called Moses to the top of the mountain, and Moses went up" (Ex. 19:20).

Through the rest of the book of Exodus, Moses speaks with God on the top of Mount Sinai, receiving the divine law and also receiving detailed instructions for constructing an elaborate, mobile tent called a "tabernacle," which would house and protect sacred items as well as serve as a temporary and portable temple. Above all, though, the tabernacle served for centuries as the dwelling place of God among his people. On the day it was completed, "The cloud covered the tent of meeting, and the glory of the LORD filled the tabernacle" (Ex. 40:34). Once again, God was present among his people.

For all the excitement of that moment, though, it quickly becomes clear that having the God of the universe live right beside you brings challenges. Several Christians have noted that it must have been like living with an armed nuclear bomb sitting right in the middle of your camp! If you do something wrong, if you offend God or don't give him the honor due to him, if you cut the blue wire instead of the red one, *boom!* Indeed, Israel experienced that explosion several times when God judged them for egregious sin by fire, plague, enemy armies, even the earth opening up to swallow some of them. So dangerous was it to have the holy presence of God dwelling among sinful people that God gave them an elaborate system of sacrifices to temporarily assuage his wrath against the wickedness and sin that continually cried out for his judgment. We'll talk more about the meaning of those sacrifices in a later chapter, but suffice it to say for now that they made it possible for a nation of sinful rebels to live in the presence of the holy God of the universe without being destroyed.

This state of affairs persisted for several hundred years until, in 2 Samuel, King David conquered the city of Jerusalem and made it his capital. By that time, the nation of Israel was united under a single crown and maturing into a regional power, and David decided it was time to upgrade God's traveling tent to a permanent house—a temple. God, however, forbade David to build it; there was simply too much blood on his hands. The task of building the temple would fall to David's son and successor, Solomon. In 2 Chronicles 6 Solomon finishes constructing the temple—a magnificently beautiful structure right in the heart of Jerusalem the capital—and prays to consecrate it to God's use. What happens next is unmistakable:

> As soon as Solomon finished his prayer, fire came down from heaven and consumed the burnt offering and the sacrifices, and the glory of the Lord filled the temple. And the priests could not enter the house of the Lord, because the glory of the Lord filled the Lord's house. When all the people of

Israel saw the fire come down and the glory of the LORD on the temple, they bowed down with their faces to the ground on the pavement and worshiped and gave thanks to the LORD, saying, "For he is good, for his steadfast love endures forever." (2 Chron. 7:1–3)

God was making it clear again. This was his people. This was his city. And this temple was his dwelling place, the place of his divine presence.

Through the centuries, the nation of Israel enjoyed enormous benefits from having God's presence dwell among them. They made sacrifices and worshiped at the temple. God promised to protect the city of Jerusalem against its enemies, as Sennacherib of Assyria learned in one fatefully tragic day when God killed 185,000 of his soldiers in a single night! The Israelites were *his* people, and he was their God.

Over time, however, the people of Israel began to misunderstand what God's presence among them really meant. They began to see the temple—and God's presence in it—as nothing more than a kind of rabbit's-foot talisman to ward off trouble, and they began to take God's presence among them for granted. The prophets Ezekiel and Jeremiah both castigate the nation for that miscalculation, reminding them that God owed them nothing. The covenant he had made with them was not unconditional, and if they broke it by worshiping pagan gods and practicing other kinds of wickedness, he would abandon them, just as he'd said at the very beginning. Ezekiel tells what happened when God finally did just that—when he abandoned the temple in Jerusalem to its fate and judgment:

Then I looked, and behold, on the expanse that was over the heads of the cherubim there appeared above them something like a sapphire, in appearance like a throne. . . . And the glory of the LORD went up from the cherub to the threshold of the house, and the house was filled with the cloud, and the court was filled with the brightness of the glory of the LORD. . . . And I looked, and behold, there were four wheels beside the cherubim, one beside each cherub, and the appearance of the wheels was like sparkling beryl. . . . And the cherubim mounted up. These were the living creatures that I saw by the Chebar canal. And when the cherubim went, the wheels went beside them. And when the cherubim lifted up their wings to mount up from the earth, the wheels did not turn from beside them. When they stood still, these stood still, and when they mounted up, these mounted up with them, for the spirit of the living creatures was in them.

Then the glory of the LORD went out from the threshold of the house, and stood over the cherubim. And the cherubim lifted up their wings and mounted up from the earth before my eyes as they went out, with the wheels beside them. And they stood at the entrance of the east gate of the house of the LORD, and the glory of the God of Israel was over them. . . .

Then the cherubim lifted up their wings, with the wheels beside them, and the glory of the God of Israel was over them. And the glory of the LORD went up from the midst of the city and stood on the mountain that is on the east side of the city. (Ezek. 10:1, 4, 9, 15–19; 11:22–23)

The imagery in that passage isn't entirely easy, and you'll learn more about "cherubim" and "wheels" and all the rest when you read Ezekiel. But if you squint your eyes just a little, you can see what's happening: the glory of the presence of the Lord mounts up on a sapphire throne on the backs of these cherubim—these "burning ones"—and moves from the center of the temple to the threshold (that is, the doorway) of what was known as the Holy of Holies, the very center of the temple where God dwelt. In other words, God is exiting the building. After a moment, the cherubim then mount up as if pulling a war chariot and carry the sapphire throne and the glory of the Lord from the threshold of the Holy of Holies out to the east gate of the temple. There the Lord pauses, as if giving the nation one more opportunity to repent and return to him, but finally, the cherubim lift up their wings and the glory of the Lord departs toward the mountains to the east of the city.

Without a doubt, this is one of the most devastating moments in the entire Bible—perhaps even its nadir. God is gone. The covenant is broken. The special relationship between him and the people of Israel is shattered, and Israel is left to suffer judgment. If you recall the flyover from the last chapter, you remember what happens next—the exile. In 586 BC, the armies of Nebuchadnezzar of Babylon swept down from the north and laid waste to the city of Jerusalem, destroying and burning the temple, looting its treasures, and ultimately taking most of the people away to exile in Babylon. This was not only a political catastrophe for Israel but a theological crisis as well. Had God been *defeated*? Were the Babylonian gods stronger than he? Had God broken his promises, or failed to deliver on them? Had God abandoned his people and his promises forever? These were the questions that the prophets Ezekiel and Daniel in particular wrestled with, and of course the answer God gave them was a resounding no! He had not failed to keep his promises; he had judged his people for their wickedness just as he had said he would. The Babylonian gods had not defeated him; he had used the Babylonian armies as his tools to carry out his own purposes. And besides that, the prophets said, God was far from finished with his people. He had not forgotten his promises.

In 536 BC, Cyrus the Persian conquered Babylon, and a year later decreed that the exiled Israelites could return to their homeland. What they saw when they arrived was heartbreaking. Broken-down walls, a ravaged city overrun with wild animals, the ruins of what had once been a beautiful and mighty temple. Under the leadership of Ezra and Nehemiah, the Israelites eventually rebuilt the wall and even the temple itself. Finally, in 516 BC—twenty years after the exiles had returned and seventy years since the temple had been destroyed, Ezra writes that the Israelites "finished their building by decree of the God of Israel and by decree of Cyrus and Darius and Artaxerxes king of Persia; and this house was finished on the third day of the month of Adar, in the sixth year of the reign of Darius the king" (Ezra 6:14–15).

This should have been—and probably was, to a certain extent—a glorious occasion. Songs were sung, feasts were kept, animals were sacrificed. But the whole thing was a humble affair compared to the consecration of the temple in Solomon's day. The one hundred bulls, two hundred rams, and four hundred lambs offered as sacrifice this time absolutely paled against the 22,000 oxen, 120,000 sheep, and countless rams Solomon had offered. Worst of all, there was no fire. The glory of the presence of the Lord didn't come. Nothing happened. Despite the fact that the prophets, especially Haggai, had promised that the Lord's presence and glory would fill this new temple, too, it didn't happen—not yet.

Restored Presence

In the 10s and aughts BC, Herod the Great—the Roman-appointed "king of Judea"—began a massive renovation and expansion of the relatively humble temple. By the year 0, it was a resplendent structure, towering over the city of Jerusalem and reflecting light from its whitewashed and gold-trimmed walls for miles around. This was the structure that God finally filled again with his presence, this time in the person of Jesus Christ. Here's what happens as John recounts it in John 2:

> The Passover of the Jews was at hand, and Jesus went up to Jerusalem. In the temple he found those who were selling oxen and sheep and pigeons, and the money-changers sitting there. And making a whip of cords, he drove them all out of the temple, with the sheep and oxen. And he poured out the coins of the money-changers and overturned their tables. And he told those who sold the pigeons, "Take these things away; do not make my Father's house a house of trade." His disciples remembered that it was written, "Zeal for your house will consume me."
>
> So the Jews said to him, "What sign do you show us for doing these things?" Jesus answered them, "Destroy this temple, and in three days I will raise it up." The Jews then said, "It has taken forty-six years to build this temple, and will you raise it up in three days?" But he was speaking about the temple of his body. (John 2:13–21)

Part of what's happening here is the fulfillment of prophecies like Malachi's that when the Lord returned to his temple this time, it would be as a refiner's fire, cleansing the temple of those who would rob God. But even more importantly, notice what Jesus does here by saying "Destroy this temple, and in three days I will raise it up" *with reference to his own body*. Do you see? He's saying that the temple is no longer the dwelling place of God; it's no longer the place where God and humans meet. Now that place is *him*. No longer is God's presence a matter of a particular building in a particular city. God's presence is found in a *person*, in Jesus Christ. Through ups and downs, glories and catastrophes, the biblical theme of God's presence finally finds its fulfillment in Jesus. He is the living presence of God, the "place" where the divine and human natures meet as one and the person to whom all must come if they would know God (John 1:14).

This point was dramatically emphasized at the moment of Jesus's sacrificial death on the cross. As Christ exhausted the decreed penalty for sin and absorbed the wrath of God, Matthew tells us that "behold, the curtain of the temple was torn in two, from top to bottom" (Matt. 27:51). The curtain of the temple was the enormous barrier (somewhere between forty-five and sixty feet high, and about six inches thick) that separated the Holy of Holies from the rest of the temple. In other words, it was a stark reminder of humanity's separation from God. But here, at the moment of Jesus's death, that barrier is torn—not from bottom to top as if humans accomplished this for themselves, but from top to bottom, *from heaven to earth*—and the way back into God's presence was thrown wide open. The great curse of Eden, mankind's separation from God, had finally been ended and reversed.

Through the rest of the New Testament, the reality that the theme of God's presence is fulfilled in Jesus develops still further, as Jesus promises that he—that is, God—will be present with his people the church until the end of time and history. So he tells them: "Behold, I am with you always, to the end of the age" (Matt. 28:20). What Jesus meant was not that he would be physically, bodily present with them. After all, his physical body ascended to heaven. What he meant was what he told them in John 14, that after his ascension to the Father's throne he would send the Holy Spirit to be with them: "I will ask the Father, and he will give you another Helper, to be with you forever, even the Spirit of truth" (John 14:16–17). In several other places, the Holy Spirit is called "the Spirit of Jesus Christ" (Phil. 1:19), "the Spirit of Jesus" (Acts 16:7), even "the Spirit of [God's] Son" (Gal. 4:6). Jesus was not mistaken; through the presence of the Holy Spirit, *his* Spirit, dwelling in their hearts, he is present with each and every one of his people *and* present with them when they gather as a church. No wonder Paul would write in 1 Corinthians 6:19, "Do you not know that your body is a temple of the Holy Spirit within you, whom you have from God?" And no wonder he would say in 1 Corinthians 3:16 *about the church*, "Do you not know that you are God's temple and that God's Spirit dwells in you?" The building is no longer the point. The dwelling place of the presence of God is now his people.

The theme of God's presence comes to its conclusion in the book of Revelation. Here's what John writes, strikingly, about the New Jerusalem:

And I saw no temple in the city, for its temple is the Lord God the Almighty and the Lamb. And the city has no need of sun or moon to shine on it, for the glory of God gives it light, and its lamp is the Lamb. By its light will the nations walk, and the kings of the earth will bring their glory into it, and its gates will never be shut by day—and there will be no night there. They will bring into it the glory and the honor of the nations. But nothing unclean will ever enter it, nor anyone who does what is detestable or false, but only those who are written in the Lamb's book of life.

Then the angel showed me the river of the water of life, bright as crystal, flowing from the throne of God and of the Lamb through the middle of the street of the city; also, on either side of the river, the tree of life with its twelve kinds of fruit, yielding its fruit each month. The leaves of the tree were for the healing of the nations. No longer will there be anything accursed, but the throne of God and of the Lamb will be in it, and his servants will worship him. They will see his face, and his name will be on their foreheads. And night will be no more. They will need no light of lamp or sun, for the Lord God will be their light, and they will reign forever and ever. (Rev. 21:22–22:5)

What a glorious end to the story! In the new Jerusalem, there is no temple, no need for one particular place where God will dwell, because he dwells right out in the open, among his people. His throne is there, and the throne of the Lamb. His people see his face, and they reign with him—joyfully in his presence, and in the presence of the Lamb Jesus Christ—forever and ever.

4

You Will Be My People

The Theme of Covenant

THOUGH NOT COMPLETELY unfamiliar to most of us, the word *covenant* doesn't often make it into our usual daily conversation. We generally know what it means because we hear it at weddings—something about the covenant of marriage—but if we were asked to define it carefully, most of us couldn't do it. Yet for all that unfamiliarity, it could be said that the entire storyline of the Bible is organized around a series of covenants that God makes with various humans. Indeed, one of the things you quickly come to see when you begin reading the Bible is that God *always* defines his relationships with human beings through covenants. So if you really want to understand the epic story of the Bible, it is critical to understand the nature of covenants and to have a basic understanding of the covenantal structure of the Bible.

Let's start with some definitions. What exactly is a *covenant*, particularly as that word is used in the Bible? One scholar has defined it like this: a covenant is "a relationship of 'oaths and bonds' and involves mutual, though not necessarily equal, commitments."[1] That's a good definition; it emphasizes the fact that a covenant is a *relationship* between two or more parties; it recognizes that a covenant is a *formal* relationship, not just a casual one; and it understands that the commitments each party makes in a covenant are not necessarily equal. While you definitely should keep that larger, fuller definition in mind, for our purposes I recommend you memorize this shorthand definition: a covenant is *a set of binding promises that two or more parties make to one another*. Essentially, that's what a marriage covenant is, right? A man and a woman stand before a congregation and they each make promises to one another—they take vows, as we say. In the making of those promises, a covenant is created between the two of them.

The interesting thing about the biblical covenants is that they show up in a variety of forms. There are certainly covenants in the Bible that are made between two humans, but the main ones—the ones that drive the story forward—are those which God himself makes with people. Sometimes God makes those covenants with individuals, sometimes with a group of people. Sometimes they come with requirements for the people engaged in them, and other times they take the form of a divine promise—a kind of *unilateral covenant* where God says without caveat or fine print, "I will do this."

Christians throughout history have often disagreed about exactly how many covenants are identifiable in the Bible, and there

---

1   Michael Horton, *God of Promise* (Grand Rapids, MI: Baker, 2006), 10.

are legitimate questions to be asked there. For example, was Adam in a covenant with God in the garden of Eden, or was that relationship something different? Should Deuteronomy be considered a separate, different covenant from the covenant created at Mount Sinai? Or should we understand all the different covenants from Abraham through the end of the story to really be one single covenant reiterated again and again through the generations? Those are excellent questions, but it's not our purpose here to answer all of those. What I want to do instead is introduce you to the major covenants that organize the Bible's storyline, familiarize you with each of them, and explain how they function to push the story along. You won't be PhD-level educated on biblical covenants after you've read this chapter. But you will be familiar enough with the unfolding covenants of the Bible that they won't scare you or throw you off when you encounter them. I hope you'll even come to see that the theme of covenant is one of the most beautiful themes of the entire Bible's epic story.

We're going to look at each of the Bible's major covenants: the covenant with Adam, the covenant with Abraham, the covenant with Israel, the covenant with David, and the new covenant.

The Covenant with Adam

Strangely enough, the word *covenant* actually doesn't show up in the Bible until Genesis 6:18, and even there it's not talking about a covenant with Adam but rather with Noah. Because of that, many biblical scholars have argued that there actually is no covenant with Adam, that God's relationship with the first humans, before they sinned, was something other than covenantal. The arguments that have been made both for and against there being a covenant in Genesis 1–3 are long and complex, but they're important too. And in the end, I think it makes the most sense to think that the biblical theme of covenant has its beginning where so many other biblical themes have theirs as well—in Eden.

Before we go any further, we should acknowledge that the fact that the word *covenant* isn't used to describe God's relationship with Adam is a strong argument, but it can't win the debate all by itself. After all, the Bible often discusses various concepts without using particular words. Look at Psalm 97, for example; clearly it's expounding on the biblical theme of God's kingship, but it never actually uses the word *king*. Instead, it uses other words and concepts to convey the reality that God is the King of creation. In the same way, though Genesis 1–3 doesn't use the word *covenant*, it may be that it uses other concepts and ideas and hints and clues to describe that reality. But the question, of course, is, does it?

I believe it does.[2] And to show you why, let's look carefully first not at the wording in Genesis 1, but in Genesis 6:18: "But I will establish my covenant with you, and you shall come into the ark, you, your sons, your wife, and your sons' wives with you."

As we've noted already, this isn't talking about Adam and Eve. Here God is telling Noah that in the wake of the great flood that will wipe out all human beings, God is going to establish his covenant with Noah in order to, essentially, start the whole human

---

2   I am indebted to my professors Peter Gentry and Stephen Wellum for teaching me the following understanding of God's covenant with Adam. You can read their full scholarly argument in chapter 6 of their book *Kingdom through Covenant: A Biblical-Theological Understanding of the Covenants* (Wheaton, IL: Crossway, 2012).

project over again. We'll talk more about that and its place in the Bible's covenantal story a bit later, but for now, look carefully at how God talks about this covenant he's making with Noah. He's *establishing* it.

No big deal, right? Well, it actually is, because the Bible uses two different words when it talks about the initiation of covenants. One of those words is the one used in Genesis 6:18, which means "to establish." The other, which might seem strange at first but will make more sense when we talk about the covenant with Abraham later, means "to *cut*" a covenant. What's the difference? The phrase "to cut a covenant" is used when there's a brand new covenant being made, while "to establish a covenant" is used when God is reaffirming a covenant that already existed. That reaffirmation may happen for a number of reasons—to bring new parties into the covenant, or because circumstances have brought the covenant into question, or even because one party has violated the covenant—but you can see why this is important for understanding God's relationship with Adam. If the covenant with Noah in Genesis 6:18 is *established* rather than *cut*, then that means that it was already in existence before Noah was brought into it! So when, then, was that covenant first *cut*? When was it first created? The most obvious answer is that the covenant God *reaffirmed* with Noah was initially *cut* . . . with Adam.

So is there anything in Genesis 1–3 that leads us to think that a covenant is being described there? There is, and it comes in the particular language of Genesis 1:26–27:

> Then God said, "Let us make man in our image, after our likeness. . . ."

So God created man in his own image,
in the image of God he created him;
male and female he created them.

The first thing to notice here is God's declaration that he is creating human beings *in his image* and *after his likeness*. The prepositions *in* and *after* aren't too important; in fact, they'll be used in the reverse order later in the Bible. Not only so, but both of them are probably best understood as meaning "as." So God declares, right from the start, that Adam and Eve will be his image and likeness in the world. This is a unique declaration; no other creature in all the cosmos is given those titles and descriptions, and given that God creates humankind *last*, it's clear that he intends for humans to be the very pinnacle of his creating work. When Adam the human had been created, God rested from his work.

But what does it mean, exactly, to say that Adam and Eve were created as God's image and likeness? Christians have debated that question for centuries, and books have been written about it. Some have argued that those two words must be referring to some kind of physical resemblance between humans and God. Others have said that they refer to certain faculties and abilities that we share with God—self-awareness, for example, or reason or will or creativity. There certainly may be something to that second argument, but I think the best understanding of humans being the *image* and *likeness* of God comes from, believe it or not, ancient Near Eastern conceptions of a ruler's relationship to their false gods.

I'm not kidding. The Bible often uses common words and phrases from the surrounding time and culture, though seldom in a one-to-one equality of meaning. When God uses common words and phrases, there are often subtle—or even glaring—differences in precisely how they're used, differences that highlight the infinite differences between the God of the Bible and the false gods of the nations. Something like that is happening when God uses the words *image* and *likeness* to describe his relationship with Adam; he's saying that it is *somewhat* like the relationship ancient Near Eastern kings thought they had with their false gods. So what was that relationship?

Most fundamentally, it was a *covenantal* relationship, one that extended in two different directions. First, to say that the king was the "likeness" of his god meant that he was in a unique, father-to-son relationship with the god that no other person on earth enjoyed. God changes this drastically when he uses the word in Genesis 1. Now it's not just one single human being who enjoys that filial relationship with God but *all* human beings! So the critical distinction is no longer between human beings—between the king and the not-kings—but between all human beings and the rest of the creation. Second, to say that the king was the "image" of his god meant that he represented and mediated the god's glory and authority to the people. The fact that he stood in a father-son relationship to a god meant that he therefore had the right to exercise the god's authority among the people—to rule them.

And here's the thing: both of those relationships—king-to-god and king-to-people—were covenantal in nature. The "god" made "promises" to the king, and the king likewise to the god—to be loyal to him and obey him. The king also was expected to rule the people with whatever virtues the god demanded, and they were expected to show the king the honor due him because of his exalted position. Faithfulness, loyalty, obedience, promises, expectations—all these are the marks of covenant relationships.

When God declares Adam and Eve to be his image and likeness, the best way to understand that is in terms of a covenant being established, both between the humans and God (to honor and obey him), and between the humans and the creation (to rule it well, just as God does). Even more, there were requirements and stipulations, as well as consequences for breaking the covenant and rewards for keeping it. So long as Adam and Eve kept the covenant—obeying God, ruling well, and protecting the purity of the garden—they had access to all the beauties and benefits of the garden of Eden. But if they broke the covenant, the natural and necessary consequence would be death.

We know well what happened in Genesis 3. Adam and Eve joined the rebellion of the serpent and broke the covenant. They were cast out of Eden, out of God's presence, and the benefits of the covenant were torn away from them. What's interesting to see, though, is that although that original covenant—the one defined by Adam and Eve's identity as the image and likeness of God—was broken, it wasn't annihilated. It was shattered and marred, and the curses of the covenant were executed, but every single human being continued (and continues to this day) to be created as the image and likeness of God. We see this again—both the persistence of that original covenant and its shattered state after Adam's sin—when we look at God's reaffirmation of the covenant with Noah.

In Genesis 6, human wickedness has reached such a fever pitch that God decides to wipe humanity out entirely—except, that is, for Noah and his family. Why is that? Because, according to Genesis 6:9, "Noah was a righteous man, blameless in his generation. Noah walked with God." If you're going to start the whole human project over again, you might as well do that with the *best* human, right? So that's what God does. He tells Noah in Genesis 6:18 that he's reaffirming his original covenant—the one he made with Adam—now with Noah, then shuts him up in the ark with a reboot menagerie and sends the floodwaters. When Noah finally emerges from his boat a year later, God speaks to him again of the covenant, but there are significant changes to it. The most significant change is God's new promise never again to "strike down every living creature" but rather to ensure that "while the earth remains" a stable, predictable rotation of "seedtime and harvest, cold and heat, summer and winter, day and night, shall not cease" (Gen. 8:21–22; see also 9:11). As a sign of that covenant promise, God placed in the sky the rainbow—a striking visual reminder that the Lord had hung up his weapon of war, never to use it for the purpose of striking down all life again.

As God lays out the details of this reestablished covenant with Noah, many of them are strikingly similar to the covenant with Adam, which underlines that this is really the same covenant but with a new head now—Noah. But even in those similarities, it's clear that something has gone terribly wrong. For example, the command God had given Adam and Eve to "be fruitful and multiply" is reestablished in Genesis 9:1, but this will no longer be a purely joyous affair; childbearing will now be marked by pain and suffering (Gen. 3:16). Also, the "dominion" Adam was given over the animals is still there in Genesis 9:2, but this too is no longer a happy thing; the animals aren't going to come meekly to Noah like they did to Adam to receive their names. Rather, "the fear of you and the dread of you shall be upon every beast of the earth." There's also the new twist of a sword-bearing, blood-shedding government, one which will have the power to take human life when human life was taken (9:6). You see what's happened here? The original covenant is still there—the command to multiply and to rule over creation—but things are clearly not the same now. Perhaps most importantly, the words from Genesis 1:28—"and subdue the earth"—are no longer there. The great goal God had given Adam—to bring the entire creation to a beautiful subjection under his and God's wonderful rule—is now out of reach. This is a changed covenant, one retooled for a fallen world, a world characterized by blood and iron.

So how does this covenant with Adam—and subsequently Noah—function in the storyline of the Bible? It actually has two critical roles. First, Adam's breaking of that original covenant through his disobedience to God is the reason all human beings live under a sentence of death. He acted as the representative of all humanity, and therefore the covenant curse of death that resulted from his rebellion hangs over us all. That death sentence, of course, finds its resolution in the life of each person either in the eternal condemnation of hell or in the sacrificial, substitutionary death of Jesus in that person's place. We'll talk more about that in chapter 6, but this point is important: the broken covenant of Adam is the first and primary reason we need to be saved. Second, the reestablished covenant with Noah really can be said to underlie all the other coming covenants. Why? Because in it, God promises to uphold the order of the world, to establish seasons and rotations, and generally to ensure that the world will be a stable, orderly stage on which the epic drama of salvation can play out.

The Covenant with Abraham

The immediate result of the flood and the reestablishment of the original covenant with Noah was simply this: to demonstrate beyond a shadow of doubt that sin's claws were sunk deep into humanity's heart. Almost immediately even Noah—Noah the righteous one, Noah the best of the best, Noah the one who walked with God—sinned and found himself in the same shameful state of nakedness that Adam experienced when he disobeyed God (Gen. 9:20–21). From there the generations pass and sin proves itself to be intractable until humans, in their immense pride, seek once again to challenge God's supremacy—not this time by eating forbidden fruit, but by literally trying to build a tower that would allow them to ascend to the height of heaven. God frustrates the plan, but it's clear that humans are still doomed—still marked by the same pride that led Adam to rebel against God, and still therefore under the curse of death.

Starting in Genesis 12, though, God begins the next big chapter in the epic story of redemption, and once again he does so—just like with Adam and Noah beforehand—by setting his attention on one single man. This time, it is a man named Abram who lived in a city called Ur in the land that would one day be ruled by the Babylonians. This means that Abram and his family were, most likely, pagans . . . until the moment God intervened and called Abram into his service. The Bible is straightforward about that moment:

> Now the LORD said to Abram, "Go from your country and your kindred and your father's house to the land that I will show you. And I will make of you a great nation, and I will bless

you and make your name great, so that you will be a blessing.
I will bless those who bless you, and him who dishonors you
I will curse, and in you all the families of the earth shall be
blessed." (Gen. 12:1–3)

Sometime later, though only four verses later in the biblical
story, Abram is traveling through the land of Canaan and the
Lord appears to him and says, "To your offspring I will give this
land" (Gen. 12:7). This is a pivotal moment in the story, because
it is the launching of God's great plan of redemption. From this
moment will flow all the other promises, all the other covenants,
all the other prophecies that will finally culminate in the salvation
of humanity through the work of Jesus Christ.

But this is a small beginning. Abram is one man with no children, no land, and no great possessions, and yet God promises
that he will one day make of Abraham a great nation and give
him all the land his eyes can see. Moreover, and most importantly,
he promises that he will, through Abraham and ultimately his
descendants, bring blessing to all the nations and families of the
earth. Those are big promises.

But notice that at this point in the story they are just promises. There's no covenant here yet, just the bare word of God.
It's intensely interesting that God's making of his covenant with
Abraham takes place in several stages through several chapters of
Genesis. Here in chapter 12, he makes promises to Abraham of
descendants, land, and blessings. But it's not until chapter 15 that
those promises take on the formal character of a covenant, and it's
here that we learn—finally!—why covenants are said to be *cut*. The
story begins abruptly with God appearing to Abram in a vision

and reiterating both who he is and what he had promised Abram. Abram asks how he can know that the Lord will indeed keep his promises, and then things take a strange and captivating turn:

[God] said to him, "Bring me a heifer three years old, a female goat three years old, a ram three years old, a turtledove, and a young pigeon." And he brought him all these, cut them in half, and laid each half over against the other. But he did not cut the birds in half. And when birds of prey came down on the carcasses, Abram drove them away.

As the sun was going down, a deep sleep fell on Abram. And behold, dreadful and great darkness fell upon him. Then the LORD said to Abram, "Know for certain that your offspring will be sojourners in a land that is not theirs and will be servants there, and they will be afflicted for four hundred years. But I will bring judgment on the nation that they serve, and afterward they shall come out with great possessions. As for you, you shall go to your fathers in peace; you shall be buried in a good old age. And they shall come back here in the fourth generation, for the iniquity of the Amorites is not yet complete."

When the sun had gone down and it was dark, behold, a smoking fire pot and a flaming torch passed between these pieces. On that day the LORD *made a covenant* with Abram, saying, "To your offspring I give this land. . . ." (Gen. 15:9–18)

So there it is! The phrase "made a covenant" in verse 18 is actually "the Lord *cut* a covenant with Abram," and you can probably see now where that image came from. When a covenant was created in the ancient Near East, it was customary for several animals to be cut in half and for the parties of the covenant to walk between them. In effect this was to say, "If I don't keep the promises of this covenant, may the very thing that happened to these animals happen to me as well." Think about it: when Abram walked between those pieces, he was saying . . . wait, no, *Abram didn't walk between them at all.* Look back at verse 17. It was a "smoking fire pot and a flaming torch," representing God himself, that walked between the pieces. That means that God is taking sole responsibility to carry out the provisions of this covenant, to do for Abram exactly what he promised. That's not to say that there was nothing required of Abraham. God expected him to trust him, to believe in him, to remain loyal to him; Genesis 22 would provide a heart-wrenchingly dramatic test of that loyalty and trust, in fact (see chap. 6). But the weight of this covenant with Abraham would be on God and God alone. He would see to it that his promises were kept.

Genesis 16 seems almost precision-engineered to test God's resolve in that matter. Abram's faith in God collapses, and instead of waiting on God to give him the offspring (the son) he had promised, Abram decides to take matters into his own hands and father a child by his wife's maidservant. It's a decision that would have consequences for Abram's descendants for centuries to come, and the question that hangs in its shadow is, "Does this mean the covenant is broken?" Chapter 17 answers that question with a resounding *no.* God comes to Abraham again:

> When Abram was ninety-nine years old the LORD appeared to Abram and said to him, "I am God Almighty; walk before me, and be blameless, that I may *make* my covenant between me

and you, and may multiply you greatly." Then Abram fell on his face. And God said to him, "Behold, my covenant is with you, and you shall be the father of a multitude of nations. No longer shall your name be called Abram, but your name shall be Abraham, for I have made you the father of a multitude of nations. I will make you exceedingly fruitful, and I will make you into nations, and kings shall come from you. And *I will establish my covenant* between me and you and your offspring after you throughout their generations for an everlasting covenant, to be God to you and to your offspring after you. And I will give to you and to your offspring after you the land of your sojournings, all the land of Canaan, for an everlasting possession, and I will be their God." (Gen. 17:1–8)

Essentially, God here confirms the covenant he had made with Abraham in chapter 15. In verse 7 he uses that meaningful phrase "I will *establish* my covenant," and the word "make" in verse 2 is a different word that yet means the same thing. Two more things are worth noticing. First, God changes Abram's name to Abraham—that is, from "exalted father" to "father of a multitude," an obvious reflection on God's promises to make of him a great nation and through him bring blessing to all the families of the earth. Second, God gives Abraham a covenant sign—circumcision—that will henceforth mark all the members of the covenant family (Gen. 17:10–14).

At this point in the story, it's not entirely clear how God intends to keep this covenant. The promise of Genesis 3:15 seems to find reflection here in God's promise—now formalized in a covenant—to bring blessing to the nations, and also in his promise in Genesis 17:6 that "kings shall come from you." The storyline is moving forward, but it remains to be seen exactly how God will keep his promise. Regardless, God's cutting of the covenant with Abraham is one of the highest mountain peaks in the entire story of the Bible. From here you can see all the way back to Eden, and you can look far ahead—through mists and dark clouds still, to be sure—but far ahead to the coming of the offspring himself, the Messiah who will bring blessing to the world.[3]

The Covenant with Israel

Did you ever as a kid play the game "Kill the Carrier"? One kid would run around with a football until the mob tackled him, then threw the football up in the air, and the kid who caught it would run around until he, too, got tackled and had to throw the ball up for grabs again. Pointless, but fun. After God's promises are reiterated to Abraham's son Isaac and then to Isaac's son Jacob, the rest of the story of Genesis becomes one giant game of "Covenantal Kill the Carrier." You see, Jacob has twelve sons, and one by one, each one of them dramatically manages to cough up the "ball" of God's promises and covenant, disqualifying himself from being the covenant head by his sin and disobedience to God. The fact that God was going to keep those promises is never once in doubt; the question is simply "Through which of these guys is he going to do it?"

By the end of Genesis, it looks for all the world like it's going to be Joseph who catches the ball. He's the second-youngest of Jacob's sons, but he rises fast—from being sold into slavery by his brothers

---

3 Paul identifies the singular "offspring" of the Abrahamic covenant as Jesus in Galatians 3:16.

because of their jealousy, to being crowned second-in-command of all Egypt, to (by the end) blessing the next generation and teaching his brothers about the ways and providence of God. Joseph's is a remarkable career. And then he's seldom heard from again. That's admittedly a jolting turn of events, but it underlines God's sovereignty in the story. What we expect or want to happen is not always what he does, and he is under no obligation to conform his actions to our expectations. We expect Joseph to be the next head and mediator of the covenant with Abraham, but God had other plans. In fact, at this point in the story, the end of Genesis and the beginning of Exodus, the covenant with Abraham recedes in focus as another covenant takes center stage—the covenant with Israel, often called the covenant with Moses.

The story of the exodus from Egypt, which runs from Exodus 1–18, is a dramatic *tour-de-force*. God quite literally goes to war with Pharaoh, himself considered to be the image and likeness of the Egyptian sun god Amon-Re. God systematically defeats all the greatest gods of Egypt, finally blotting out Amon-Re himself when the sun goes dark in the ninth plague. With regard to the theme of covenant, what is notable is that God's move to redeem his people from slavery in Egypt was *explicitly* an action in keeping with the covenant he'd made with Abraham. He says so in Exodus 2:24: "And God heard their groaning, and God remembered his covenant with Abraham, with Isaac, and with Jacob." And he tells Moses the same thing in Exodus 6:4–5: "I also established my covenant with them to give them the land of Canaan, the land in which they lived as sojourners. Moreover, I have heard the groaning of the people of Israel whom the Egyptians hold as slaves, and I have remembered my covenant."

So God goes to war for his people in fulfillment of the covenant he had made with them.

Then starting in Exodus 19, the theme of covenant in the Bible's storyline takes another major step forward. There the Lord gathers the people of Israel to a mountain in the wilderness of Egypt, calls Moses to the top of the mountain, and invites Israel to make a covenant with him, to be his people even as he will be their God. The story of the cutting of that covenant is told in Exodus 24:

> Moses came and told the people all the words of the LORD and all the rules. And all the people answered with one voice and said, "All the words that the LORD has spoken we will do." And Moses wrote down all the words of the LORD. He rose early in the morning and built an altar at the foot of the mountain, and twelve pillars, according to the twelve tribes of Israel. And he sent young men of the people of Israel, who offered burnt offerings and sacrificed peace offerings of oxen to the LORD. And Moses took half of the blood and put it in basins, and half of the blood he threw against the altar. Then he took the Book of the Covenant and read it in the hearing of the people. And they said, "All that the LORD has spoken we will do, and we will be obedient." And Moses took the blood and threw it on the people and said, "Behold the blood of the covenant that the LORD has made [cut] with you in accordance with all these words." (Ex. 24:3–8)

This was a solemn moment—a sinful, rebellious nation cutting a covenant with the great God of the universe, to become his special people out of all the nations of the earth. At its most fundamental level, God's making a covenant like this was an act of incredible grace. He didn't have to bind himself in covenant with this nation; in fact, even if he'd wanted to choose a nation that was descended from Abraham, it didn't have to be the descendants of Jacob. He could have chosen a nation descended from Esau (Jacob's brother) or even Ishmael (Isaac's illegitimate brother). Moreover, it wasn't as if the nation of Israel was the most powerful or the largest; no, God chose them simply because he loved them, and out of all the nations of the earth, he wanted them to be *his*.

And his intentions for Israel were glorious:

> You yourselves have seen what I did to the Egyptians, and how I bore you on eagles' wings and brought you to myself. Now therefore, if you will indeed obey my voice and keep my covenant, you shall be my treasured possession among all peoples, for all the earth is mine; and you shall be to me a kingdom of priests and a holy nation. (Ex. 19:4–6)

Sitting at the crossroads of the world—right between the empires of Egypt, Assyria, and Babylon—the nation of Israel would be a kingdom of priests who would show all the peoples of the world the ways and character of God. They would therefore, as God put it to Abraham, be a blessing to all the families of the earth and ultimately from them would come the offspring who would win salvation for the world.

So how does the covenant with Israel relate to the covenant with Abraham? It's not the same covenant; it has different terms, stipulations, and ends. But as we've seen, the covenant with Abraham very much underlies the covenant with Israel. It is the reason God saved Israel and brought them into covenant with himself. And the covenant with Israel is also probably best understood as being the specific means by which God would keep the promises of the covenant with Abraham. Think of it like this: Do you remember the three main promises God made to Abraham? To give him land, offspring, and ultimately to bring blessing to the entire world through him. It is through the covenant with Israel that God ultimately does all three of those things. He gives Israel the Promised Land (and ultimately, the new Jerusalem). He makes Israel a great nation, literally giving Abraham millions of offspring, and then ultimately bringing *the* offspring—the Messiah—from them. Then through that offspring of Abraham, God blesses the world with the gift of salvation. Ultimately, God chooses to fulfill the covenant with Abraham through the covenant with Israel. Thus the covenant with Israel is a great engine by which the work of redemption and the epic story of the Bible are driven forward.

The Covenant with David

Having read this far in this book, you know what to expect next on the trail. It becomes clear through the book of Deuteronomy that the covenant with Israel is not in any sense a unilateral covenant. Moses articulates both blessings and curses that will obtain depending on whether Israel maintains her faithfulness to the covenant or not. Through the book of Judges and the first part of 1 Samuel, it becomes clear that they will not; Israel repeatedly breaks the stipulations of the covenant, to the point that God would be perfectly justified in executing the covenant curses against them. And yet, in grace and mercy, he forbears.

In the books of Samuel, the theme of covenant in the epic story takes its next great step forward. We'll save the details of how and why Israel found herself with a king in the first place for the next chapter. What's important for our purposes now is to see that once kingship was established in Israel, and once David had assumed the throne, God moved to cut yet another covenant—this time with David himself. The key text is 2 Samuel 7:1–17:

Now when the king lived in his house and the LORD had given him rest from all his surrounding enemies, the king said to Nathan the prophet, "See now, I dwell in a house of cedar, but the ark of God dwells in a tent." And Nathan said to the king, "Go, do all that is in your heart, for the LORD is with you."

But that same night the word of the LORD came to Nathan, "Go and tell my servant David, 'Thus says the LORD: Would you build me a house to dwell in? I have not lived in a house since the day I brought up the people of Israel from Egypt to this day, but I have been moving about in a tent for my dwelling. In all places where I have moved with all the people of Israel, did I speak a word with any of the judges of Israel, whom I commanded to shepherd my people Israel, saying, "Why have you not built me a house of cedar?" Now, therefore, thus you shall say to my servant David, "Thus says the LORD of hosts, I took you from the pasture, from following the sheep, that you should be prince over my people Israel. And I have been with you wherever you went and have cut off all your enemies from before you. And I will make for you a great name, like the name of the great ones of the earth. And I will appoint a place for my people Israel and will plant them, so that they may dwell in their own place and be disturbed no more. And violent men shall afflict them no more, as formerly, from the time that I appointed judges over my people Israel. And I will give you rest from all your enemies. Moreover, the LORD declares to you that the LORD will make you a house. When your days are fulfilled and you lie down with your fathers, I will raise up your offspring after you, who shall come from your body, and I will establish his kingdom. He shall build a house for my name, and I will establish the throne of his kingdom forever. I will be to him a father, and he shall be to me a son. When he commits iniquity, I will discipline him with the rod of men, with the stripes of the sons of men, but my steadfast love will not depart from him, as I took it from Saul, whom I put away from before you. And your house and your kingdom shall be made sure forever before me. Your throne shall be established forever.""" In accordance with all these words, and in accordance with all this vision, Nathan spoke to David.

The immediate story is that David has conquered Jerusalem and united the warring tribes of Israel into one nation. The previous king, Saul, is dead and the crown is David's without rival. Once David conquered Jerusalem and made it his capital, though, his people set themselves to the task of building a palace for him. David realized the incongruity of this—himself living in a palace of cedar while his God had a tent for a dwelling place—and inquired of the prophet Nathan about the possibility of building God a house more fitting for him. Nathan initially agreed, but the Lord came to him that night and forbade David to build him a house. Instead, God said he himself would build *David* a house—not a physical one, but a royal dynasty that would last forever. He promised David that he would make a "great name" for him, that he would give his people "a place," and ultimately that his "throne shall be established forever."

A few things are worth noting here. First, the word *covenant* is never used in 2 Samuel 7. However, other places in the Bible clearly refer to what happens here as the cutting of a covenant between God and David (2 Sam. 23:5; 2 Chron. 13:5; Jer. 33:21; Pss. 89:3, 28, 34, 39; 132:12; Isa. 55:3). Second, this is yet another narrowing of the *means* by which God would keep the promises of his covenant with Abraham; now it's not through the nation of Israel but specifically through the *king* of the nation of Israel that God will keep those promises. The promise of land is reiterated in the promise of "a place" (2 Sam. 7:10); the promise of offspring in a promise of "offspring" (7:12); and the promise of blessing in the promise that "your throne shall be established forever" (7:16). Third, notice that this covenant has elements that both make it clear that God will bring its promises to pass *and* that call the king and his descendants to remain faithful to God. You can see this balance clearly in 2 Samuel 7:14–16:

> I will be to him a father, and he shall be to me a son. When he commits iniquity, I will discipline him with the rod of men, with the stripes of the sons of men, but my steadfast love will not depart from him, as I took it from Saul, whom I put away from before you. And your house and your kingdom shall be made sure forever before me.

The king is expected to obey God and remain loyal to him and, if he doesn't, there will be consequences. Yet in the end, God's steadfast love—his covenant love—will not depart from him, and God will unfailingly keep his promises. Ultimately, God's everlasting covenant with Abraham—to bring blessing to the nations through his offspring—will be fulfilled through a King of Israel who will sit on David's throne forever.

The New Covenant

By 586 BC, all of those promises of God seemed to be hopelessly lost and defunct. Most of the nation of Israel had been dissolved over a century earlier into the Assyrian Empire, and now the people of Jerusalem were being carried away into exile by the armies of the Babylonian King Nebuchadnezzar, their capital city in flames and the temple of the living God destroyed. But the situation was even worse than that. See, in the covenant with David, God had committed himself to fulfilling all the promises of the covenant with Abraham through a Davidic king—one of David's descendants. But here's how the Bible tells of the fate of the last king of Israel, a puppet named Zedekiah:

> The army of the Chaldeans pursued the king and overtook Zedekiah in the plains of Jericho, and all his army was scattered from him. Then they captured the king and brought him up to the king of Babylon at Riblah in the land of Hamath, and he passed sentence on him. The king of Babylon slaughtered the sons of Zedekiah before his eyes, and also slaughtered all the officials of Judah at Riblah. He put out the eyes of Zedekiah, and bound him in chains, and the king of Babylon took him to Babylon, and put him in prison till the day of his death. (Jer. 52:8–11)

Utter disaster! Not only was the last king of Israel dragged off to die in exile in Babylon, but the very last thing he saw before Nebuchadnezzar commanded his eyes to be put out was his sons being slaughtered before him. In other words, the royal line of David was being completely cut off and snuffed out. But hadn't God said that all the promises he'd made to Abraham would be fulfilled through a royal descendant of David? Hadn't he made it clear that the great promised king of Genesis 3:15 would be one from the line of David? How could this be, now that David's line lay dead at Riblah?

By the time Zedekiah watched his sons die, all the covenants God had made with his people were in ruins. Sure, the covenant with Noah still stood; morning and evening continued to come in their order, and the seasons in theirs. But the covenants through which God intended to save humanity seemed utterly lost. The covenant with Israel was irreparably broken, its curses executed as foreign armies marched through the land and wild beasts reclaimed the rubble of Jerusalem. The covenant with David, too, seemed wrecked, along with the covenant with Abraham. Sure, God had promised that he would bring those promises to pass, but that covenant depended on a Davidic King to bring it to fulfillment, and there was no longer a Davidic King. The real tragedy, then, of the destruction of Jerusalem by the Babylonians wasn't just the suffering of the people, as awful as it was; it was the apparent catastrophic failure of God's covenants.

Into this cataclysm, though, a new group of men began to speak words of hope coming after judgment. These were the prophets— Isaiah, Jeremiah, Ezekiel, Daniel, and the others. Through sermons, poems, oracles, and acted-out illustrations, they proclaimed the message that God was not done with his people; he wasn't abandoning the promises of his covenants. In fact, they said, even in the shadow of the broken covenant with Israel, God was about to act again—this time to make a new covenant that would bring both the covenant with Abraham and the covenant with David to glorious fulfillment.

The Old Testament prophets speak of this new covenant at least thirteen different times, and by various names. Sometimes it is an everlasting covenant, sometimes a covenant of peace, and once it is called specifically, by Jeremiah, "a new covenant." Here's what God says through him:

> Behold, the days are coming, declares the LORD, when I will make a new covenant with the house of Israel and the house of Judah, not like the covenant that I made with their fathers on the day when I took them by the hand to bring them out of the land of Egypt, my covenant that they broke, though I was their husband, declares the LORD. For this is the covenant that I will make with the house of Israel after those days, declares the LORD: I will put my law within them, and I will write it on their hearts. And I will be their God, and they shall be my people. And no longer shall each one teach his neighbor and each his brother, saying, "Know the LORD," for they shall all know me, from the least of them to the greatest, declares the LORD. For I will forgive their iniquity, and I will remember their sin no more. (Jer. 31:31–34)

It's important to notice that the Lord sharply contrasts this new covenant with "the covenant I made with their fathers on the day when I took them by the hand to bring them out of the land of Egypt." That was the covenant with Israel, and it is called here "my covenant which they broke." So this is not a reestablishing of that old covenant. It is, as verse 31 makes clear, the cutting of a brand new one. That fact is clear, too, in the stark differences that exist between the broken covenant and this new one. Where the law of the broken covenant had been written on stone tablets, in the new covenant it will be written on the hearts of those who are included in it. Most gloriously, there will no longer be any threatening covenant curses for sin, for—somehow, in some way—God will forgive his people's iniquity and remember their sin no more.

Other prophets shine more light on exactly how God would do that, and it turns out that it would be through the sacrificial work of a King of Israel, one in the line and dynasty of David. We'll talk more about how that could happen, especially in the light of Zedekiah's and his sons' deaths, in the next chapter. For now, it's enough to see the central role the Davidic King plays in the fulfillment of the new covenant. One of the most important passages in this regard is Isaiah 52–53, which tells of a figure known as the servant of the Lord who secures his people's forgiveness by being punished in their place—taking their wounds as his own, enduring their suffering, and ultimately dying in their stead—and then, somehow, living again even after his own death.

The new covenant and all its blessings—intimate knowledge of and relationship with God, a new heart on which the law of God is written, even the forgiveness of sins—will be built and founded on the saving actions of a future Davidic King.

Ezekiel too seems to recognize this, when he places the Davidic King at the very center of the reconstituted new covenant people of God:

> My servant David shall be king over them, and they shall all have one shepherd. They shall walk in my rules and be careful to obey my statutes. They shall dwell in the land that I gave to my servant Jacob, where your fathers lived. They and their children and their children's children shall dwell there forever, and David my servant shall be their prince forever. I will make a covenant of peace with them. It shall be an everlasting covenant with them. And I will set them in their land and multiply them, and will set my sanctuary in their midst forevermore. My dwelling place shall be with them, and I will be their God, and they shall be my people. Then the nations will know that I am the LORD who sanctifies Israel, when my sanctuary is in their midst forevermore. (Ezek. 37:24–28)

What an incredible passage! Not only does it promise that David (by which the prophet means a descendant of David) will be king in the midst of the people of this new, everlasting covenant of peace, but it also foretells the restoration of everything that seemed so hopelessly lost. The dynasty of David is restored, the people are set in the land and made a great nation once more, and gloriously above all, the Lord dwells once again with his people—his sanctuary is in their midst forevermore!

It would be almost six hundred years before Ezekiel's words came to fulfillment. In the upper room of a house in Jerusalem Jesus—the one called Christ, as a descendant of King David—

declared that the new covenant was finally being inaugurated. The last act of God's plan to save humanity from sin was about to begin. Here's what Jesus said on that night, as recorded by Luke:

> And when the hour came, he reclined at table, and the apostles with him. And he said to them, "I have earnestly desired to eat this Passover with you before I suffer. For I tell you I will not eat it until it is fulfilled in the kingdom of God." . . . And he took bread, and when he had given thanks, he broke it and gave it to them, saying, "This is my body, which is given for you. Do this in remembrance of me." And likewise the cup after they had eaten, saying, "This cup that is poured out for you is the new covenant in my blood." (Luke 22:14–16, 19–20)

Matthew records that Jesus was even more specific about the purpose of this new covenant: "And he took a cup, and when he had given thanks he gave it to them, saying, "Drink of it, all of you, for this is my blood of the covenant, which is poured out for many for the forgiveness of sins" (Matt. 26:27–28).

Finally, after all the centuries, God's promise of a new covenant, one which would never be broken because it was secured by the blood of the eternal Davidic King, was being kept once and for all.

In the years after Jesus's death, resurrection, and ascension to heaven, his apostles clarified the meaning of the new covenant. Unlike the old one, this covenant was not exclusive to one nation or family. Rather, it was centered and founded upon the life and work of the King who secured it, and everyone, without exception, who was united to that King in faith and trust would be included in it.

The covenant theme comes to its ultimate fulfillment at the end of the book of Revelation, when the new Jerusalem descends from heaven and a loud voice from heaven cries out, "Behold, the dwelling place of God is with man. He will dwell with them, and they will be his people, and God himself will be with them as their God" (Rev. 21:3). Those are not just any words; they are the covenantal refrain that has rung through the pages of the Old Testament since the very beginning, the great hope toward which all the covenants ultimately were straining. And, here at the end in the city of the great King, they have finally and forever been fulfilled, never again to be broken because they are secured and guaranteed by the life and power of Jesus the risen King.

5

The Lord's Anointed

The Theme of Kingship

YOU ARE PROBABLY already noticing that the various themes that weave in and through the storyline of the Bible are not at all independent of one another. In many ways they build on each other and reinforce one another, much as the various strands of a rope are not one and the same, but weave around one another and thereby strengthen one another. For example, the theme of God's presence is tightly bound up with the theme of covenant because it is precisely by putting himself in covenant with his people that God comes to dwell with them, and it is by the breaking of that covenant that the people forfeit God's presence. Similarly, at the end of the last chapter it became obvious that the theme of covenant was becoming tightly bound up with the theme of this chapter—kingship. Indeed once God inaugurated the Davidic covenant, the kingship became the sole and very means by which the covenants—all of them—would be brought to fulfillment.

Another thing you've probably begun to notice, as we've been tracing these themes, is that we tend to return repeatedly to the same mountaintop texts. That's not super surprising. After all, as in any epic story, some moments in the Bible's narrative manage to push several themes forward all at the same time. In fact, those moments are recognized as the highest and most important points of the story. The creation of human beings in Genesis 1 and their fall into sin in Genesis 3, for example, are the launching points for virtually all of the Bible's greatest themes. In the same way, the cutting of the covenant with David pushes forward both covenant and kingship. And it's not surprising—in fact it's the whole point of the entire epic story—that all the great themes of the Bible find their landing place in the life and person of Jesus Christ.

So the themes of the Bible's storyline are deeply interrelated and mutually reinforcing. But I hope you're also learning that their interrelatedness does not mean that they are indistinguishable. Each of the themes we're tracing in this book—and others that we are not—has its own unique course, its own distinctive shape and direction and development that readers of the Bible can trace individually. And even though the various themes often share some of the grand story's high points—they meet, at times, on well-known mountaintops—each of them also has high points all its own, moments in the story that uniquely and specially push that theme forward. All that speaks to the beautiful richness and multilayered complexity of the Bible; you really could read it from start to finish a dozen times and, depending on which theme you've chosen to trace, feel like you've embarked on a new—if related—adventure. And yet again, none of those themes stands alone. They all weave and fold together into the one grand and epic story of the Bible.

I say all that now because in this chapter, and even more in the next, you'll start to see more clearly how the Bible's themes interact with one another and layer on top of each other, how they exert pressure on each other and push each other onward. In fact, you could even argue that the theme this chapter traces—kingship—is the central theme in the story, the one without which the others simply cannot cohere. The significance of the kingship theme is apparent even in the most common appellation given to Jesus in the New Testament: he is Jesus *Christ*, which is not (contrary to far too much common misunderstanding!) his last name, but rather his title. "Christ" is simply the Greek translation of the Hebrew word *Messiah*, which originally meant "anointed one" and could apply to anyone who was anointed with oil, but which eventually became a descriptor of the most central anointed one of all—the king. So "Jesus Christ" simply means (in a Rohan-sounding kind of way), "Jesus King." That's where the theme of kingship ends, glittering on the royal brow of the King of kings.

The Garden Needs a King

But it begins, unsurprisingly, in Eden. In the last chapter we looked at Genesis 1:26–28, God's declaration that he was going to create human beings as his image and likeness. There we saw that both those words are covenantal in nature, *likeness* referring to a father-son relationship between God and humans and *image* referring to humanity's right and responsibility (by virtue of that father-son relationship) to rule creation under God. That responsibility to rule is made explicit in verse 26, where God says, "And let them have dominion over the fish of the sea and over the birds of the heavens and over the livestock and over all the earth and over every creeping thing that creeps on the earth," and then again in verse 28 when he reiterates the same idea: "And God said to them, 'Be fruitful and multiply and fill the earth and subdue it, and have dominion over the fish of the sea and over the birds of the heavens and over every living thing that moves on the earth.'" The word *dominion* in those verses is just what it sounds like. As the one who, uniquely among all created beings, has been created as God's likeness and image, Adam's very job (and Eve would shortly join him in this) was to rule creation—starting in Eden, but eventually extending out from there until the whole world is "subdued" under his, and therefore God's, rule.

If you think about it, the work God was doing here was beautiful. He was building a structure of authority into his creation wherein Adam and Eve would rule over the rest of creation, Adam would exercise leadership in his relationship with Eve, and ruling over it all in high splendor would be the Creator himself, the Lord, the high King of the universe. It's important to see here that although God gave Adam and Eve "dominion" over creation, their rule was not ultimate. If God was the high King, they were merely his vice-regents, and therefore their authority and dominion were derived; they were secondary; and they were therefore limited. That's the meaning of the tree God set in the middle of the garden, and the reason he told Adam and Eve that they could not eat of its fruit. It was a reminder to them that there was a higher crown than their own, a higher ruler who could command and limit them.

That tree, though—called in Genesis 2 "the tree of the knowledge of good and evil"—had another purpose as well. You may remember from chapter 2 that the instructions God gave Adam when he placed him in Eden were to *abad* and *shamar* it—that is, to "work" it and "guard" it. That word *shamar* ("guard"), in particular, is critical for understanding Adam's royal position and responsibility in the garden. As king in the garden, he was to protect it, to prevent anything impure or evil from entering it, and if it did, to judge the evil thing and cast it out. Besides being a reminder of the limits of his authority, the tree of the knowledge of good and evil was also a reminder to Adam of this responsibility to guard and protect from evil. "To know good and evil," to discern the difference and judge between them, was a common way of describing the work of a king. In 2 Samuel 14:17, for example, a woman from the town of Tekoa comes to David for help, and explains why she came: "Your servant thought, 'The word of my lord the king will set me at rest,' for my lord the king is like the angel of God to discern good and evil. The LORD your God be with you!" Similarly, in 1 Kings 3:9 when Solomon is about to take the burdens of the kingship, he prays, "Give your servant therefore an understanding mind to govern your people, that I may discern between good and evil, for who is able to govern this your great people?"

What this means, then, is that the tree of the knowledge of good and evil wasn't simply some magical plant that made a person all-knowing. It was, rather, something like "the tree where good and evil are discerned." It was the judgment seat of King Adam. So it's not coincidental that when Satan comes to Adam and Eve, he comes to them while they are seated under this particular tree. This is a time for Adam to exercise his kingship, and Eve her queenship—to recognize the evil that the serpent represents, to judge it, and to cast it out of the garden entirely. Far from doing that, though, Adam and Eve both followed the serpent's lead in twisting their judgment and discernment so completely that they judged God to be the evil one, God to be in the wrong, and they joined the serpent in his rebellion. Essentially, in eating the fruit that God had forbidden them, Adam and Eve declared that they would not have his authority over them. They looked to the high King and said, by action if not in word, "You will not rule us. We will take the crown for ourselves." By that action, Adam failed utterly and catastrophically at his responsibility as king, and when he fell, he took the whole of humanity down with him.

The consequences of Adam joining the serpent's rebellion against heaven were cataclysmic. The Lord found them hiding in shame in the garden and handed down curses against all three—the serpent, the man, and the woman. No longer would life on earth be a paradise for them, but rather a hard, frustrating existence. Worst of all, their relationship with God was severed. Physical death would come later but, spiritually speaking, they died immediately—cut off from the life that can come only from being in the presence of the covenant God. Then God drove Adam and Eve out of the garden and stationed at its entrance an angel with instructions to—fascinatingly—"guard" (*shamar*) the way to the tree of life (Gen. 3:24). Do you sense the bitter irony in the use of that particular word? To *shamar* the garden had been Adam's job, but he had failed to do it. So if the vice-regent wouldn't *shamar* the garden, God would simply do it himself.

As Adam and Eve stumbled away from the garden, the flaming sword of the guardian angel flashing behind them, all seemed lost. But it wasn't. In the midst of the cataclysm, almost buried in the avalanche of curses that God poured out on Adam and Eve and the serpent, God had also made a promise. Recorded in Genesis 3:15, it's one of the most important sentences in the Bible. Speaking to the serpent, he said:

> I will put enmity between you and the woman,
>   and between your offspring and her offspring;
> he shall bruise your head,
>   and you shall bruise his heel.

To put it simply, God promises Satan that he hasn't won. Though Satan had convinced Adam to join his rebellion, one day God would send someone else, a descendant of the woman, to do what Adam should have done—crush the serpent's head. The word *king* isn't used here, but it's clear that the very role of this "offspring of the woman" will be to exercise the kingly dominion that Adam failed to. He'll pick up the sword that Adam dropped, slay the enemy that Adam allied with, and win the battle that Adam lost. In other words, he'll be the King that Adam failed to be.

Plot Twists

From that moment, a critical theme in the Bible's unfolding epic is that people begin to wonder when this promised Savior-King will come, and who it will be. So the recurring question becomes, "Which one of the descendants of Eve will be the one to set everything right?" Is it Cain? No, apparently not. Lamech? Absolutely not. Noah? His father certainly seemed to think so, rejoicing at his birth, "Out of the ground that the LORD has cursed, this one shall bring us relief from our work and from the painful toil of our hands" (Gen. 5:29). But of course it wasn't to be. God started over with Noah, but the effects of sin persisted, and the promise of Genesis 3:15 remained unfulfilled. What's striking in all this, though, is that the hope of Genesis 3:15 isn't just the coming of a King, but the coming of a King *who will reverse death and the curse.* Exactly how he's going to do that is still very cloudy at this point, but even this early in the story the good news proclaimed in Genesis is not just that a King is coming. It's that the arrival of the King *will mean salvation.* It will mean an end to the curse, and a reversal of the death and separation from God that resulted from sin. That's what the King does. He saves.

Through next few chapters of Genesis, the Genesis 3:15 promise focuses on one man, Abraham, and the nation that God would ultimately make of him. Most importantly, it is from Abraham that the promised offspring will come. (Gen. 12:7 uses the exact same word for "seed" or "offspring" as Gen. 3:15 and, strangely for the context and therefore tellingly—as Paul would later notice—it uses the *singular* form of it.) Abraham's son Isaac, though, proves not to be him, nor Isaac's son Jacob. Perhaps it's Reuben or Simeon or Levi or Judah. No, each of them in his own way seems to disqualify himself from carrying, much less fulfilling, the promise. The end of Genesis is one of the great literary head-fakes of all history, because for fifteen chapters the book does its dead-level best to convince you Joseph is going to be the fulfillment of Genesis 3:15. After all, not only is Joseph his father's favorite, not only is he pure and righteous and obviously blessed by the favor of God, but the guy *actually winds up being a kind of king*!

But then comes a stunning twist. In Genesis 49, old Jacob is offering one last prophetic blessing to his sons. As expected, Reuben receives a verbal beating, as do Simeon and Levi, and given the course of the story we're expecting the same fate for Judah. But as Jacob lays his hand on Judah's head, he says something completely unexpected:

> The scepter shall not depart from Judah,
> > nor the ruler's staff from between his feet,
> until tribute comes to him;
> > and to him shall be the obedience of the peoples.
> > (Gen. 49:10)

Contrary to everything we've been led to expect, it's not Joseph who will fulfill the promise of a coming king. It's Judah, despite the fact that we were quite sure he'd been disqualified back in Genesis 38! No, Judah himself wouldn't be the king, but one of his descendants will fulfill the promise.

Through the rest of the Pentateuch (the first five books of the Bible), God keeps promising his people that the king is coming. In Numbers 24, for example, even a pagan sorcerer named Balaam points to the future and says,

> I see him, but not now;
> > I behold him, but not near.
> a star shall come out of Jacob,
> and a scepter shall rise out of Israel; . . .
> And one from Jacob shall exercise dominion.
> > (Num. 24:17, 19)

In Deuteronomy 17, God even lays down laws to regulate the powers and responsibilities of the future king.

For all that, though, the fulfillment of the promise is long in coming, and by the end of Judges, the refrain that echoes through the rank chaos and wickedness of the people makes the reader wonder if God's promise had failed: "There was no king in Israel." In the books of Samuel Israel finally gets a king, and though the great question *"Is this him?"* is still at the forefront of the nation's mind, it turns out that none of the kings was the long-promised one of Genesis 3:15. Still, though, God used the various kings of Israel to teach the people a critical lesson. The story of 1 and 2 Samuel, on its face, is simply the story of how the nation of Israel got a king. But underneath and within that story is another, deeper one—the story of how God was teaching his people what kingship in Israel was all about, and therefore teaching them about the nature and mission of the coming one.

Israel's Kings

The story of Israel finally getting a king is told in 1 Samuel 8 and 9. Samuel himself—who played the dual role of being both a judge and a prophet of Israel—had been governing the nation for many years, but in his old age had tried to appoint his own sons to succeed him. This turned out badly, so the elders of the people gathered together at a place called Ramah and made their demand of Samuel. They said to him, "Behold, you are old and your sons do not walk in your ways. Now appoint for us a king to judge us like all the nations" (1 Sam. 8:5). The request for a king left Samuel none too happy, and he told them as much in a speech that warned of all the excesses and tyrannies a king could eventually impose. Samuel's response has left many readers wondering if the Israelites were wrong in asking for a king to rule them, if this was somehow a departure from God's plan. But surely that can't be. After all, God had promised his people many times that he would eventually give them a king. There was the prophecy of Balaam in Numbers and the regulations laid down in Deuteronomy. Not only so, but even Samuel's mother, Hannah, had prophesied that the Lord "will give strength to his king and exalt the horn of his anointed" (1 Sam. 2:10). Kingship was part of the plan all along.

So what's the problem? Why is Samuel so displeased by the people's request for a king? And for that matter, why does God himself seem unhappy with the idea when he tells Samuel, "They have not rejected you, but they have rejected me from being king over them" (1 Sam. 8:7)? The answer is that Samuel and the Lord were not upset with the Israelites for requesting a king; they were upset with *the kind of king* the Israelites requested. Kingship in Israel was always supposed to recognize the higher and ultimate kingship of God himself. The Israelite king would acknowledge that he was only a vice-regent of the high King, and he would submit himself to God's rule and seek to obey, follow, and trust in him. But that wasn't the kind of king the Israelites asked for. They asked for a king "like all the nations" (1 Sam. 8:5), one who would see himself as the ultimate ruler, the final authority, and the great protector of the people. In 1 Samuel 8:20, they even make it clear why God says they have rejected him. We want a king, they said, so "that we also may be like all the nations, and that our king may judge us and go out before us and fight our battles." There was the heart of the matter: Israel should have trusted God to fight their battles, to protect them, to go before them. He had done it before, without fail. But instead of trusting him and acknowledging his kingship over them, they wanted to be like the nations; they wanted to put their trust in a king to fight for them.

The story for the rest of the book of 1 Samuel, then, is of God teaching his people the folly of their desire and showing them instead what kingship in Israel should really be. He chooses a man named Saul to be king—a man who looks every bit the part of a king like all the nations, but who ultimately turns out to be a disaster. In the end, he disobeys God because of his foolish pride and his deference to the people, and God strips the kingdom away from him. Even as Saul's downward trajectory becomes clear, though, the story focuses on a young man named David, and before long it's obvious that he is destined for the throne. Not only so, but it's also obvious that he will be a very different king than Saul. Whereas Saul was a disastrous "king like all the nations," David was "a man after [God's] own heart" (1 Sam. 13:14), a man who—even crowned with kingly honor and authority—would remember his place before God.

The story of David and Goliath in 1 Samuel 17 is one of the most famous in the entire Bible, but the reason for its significance is not what most people think. Far from being a story about "brave little David," it is actually a brilliant drama in which God contrasts "a king like all the nations" with a king after his own heart. The picture is stark. Faced with a giant named Goliath taunting the armies of Israel, King Saul—who was specifically chosen because the people thought he'd be able to fight the nation's battles—cowered in his tent in fear. Meanwhile, young David does precisely what a king of Israel ought to do. Motivated by faith in the Lord—not his own bravery—he confronts the giant:

Then David said to the Philistine, "You come to me with a sword and with a spear and with a javelin, but I come to you in the name of the LORD of hosts, the God of the armies of Israel, whom you have defied. This day the LORD will deliver you into my hand, and I will strike you down and cut off your head. And I will give the dead bodies of the host of the Philistines this day to the birds of the air and to the wild beasts of the earth, that all the earth may know that there is a God in Israel, and that all this assembly may know that the LORD saves not with sword and spear. For the battle is the LORD's, and he will give you into our hand." (1 Sam. 17:45–47)

The point of the story is not that David was brave and Saul a coward, still less that you and I should confront our own giants with bravery. The point is that through David's actions, God was teaching Israel about the kind of king he wanted for them—one who would act in the power and name of the Lord, one who would acknowledge that the battles the king fought on the nation's behalf were ultimately not his own but the Lord's. Saul had never understood that, and when a real challenge came, he proved that he was not the kind of king Israel should ever have wanted.

After the defeat of Goliath, the heart of Israel began to move away from Saul and toward David, and it was a foregone conclusion that God had appointed David to take the throne. David's road to the crown was a rocky one, though. He spent years first in Saul's service and then on the run (living in caves and even in enemy territory for a time), but finally in about 1000 BC, the people of the tribe of Judah gathered to David at the town of Hebron—the burial place of Abraham—and crowned him king of Judah. It was two years later, after the defeat of a rival king whom the northern tribes had proclaimed, that David was crowned king of all Israel.

David reigned over Israel for forty years and brought unity and prosperity to the nation. He moved his capital from Hebron to Jerusalem, and with great rejoicing brought the ark of the covenant to its home there. David was a good king, the kind of king God intended from the start, and in 2 Samuel 7 God cut with him the covenant we saw in the previous chapter of this book—including the promise that his dynasty would last forever. For all that, though, David turned out not to be the fulfillment of the promise of Genesis 3:15. He certainly was a kind of blurry picture of the promised King, but he wasn't *him* to whom the scepter belonged. He didn't set everything right, and in fact he showed himself to be just as much under the thrall of sin as any other man. He committed adultery (or perhaps even rape; the story is ambiguous), and then murdered the husband of the woman, Bathsheba. By the end of his life, David's family was in rebellion against him, with Adonijah his son trying to usurp the throne while his dying father was kept warm in bed by a beautiful woman. Obviously, for all the good David had done, the serpent's head remained uncrushed.

The situation never really improved much from there. Adonijah's usurpation never really stood a chance, and once David proclaimed his son Solomon to be his rightful heir, Adonijah gave up his pretensions. Solomon enjoyed a brief but intense golden age. The Lord blessed him with otherworldly wisdom and the nation with untold prosperity, so much in fact that rulers of other lands took pilgrimages just to see the glories of Solomon's treasure houses. But the golden age was to be short-lived, for Solomon forgot the ancient instruction of Deuteronomy 17:

Only [the king] must not acquire many horses for himself or cause the people to return to Egypt in order to acquire many horses, since the LORD has said to you, 'You shall never return that way again.' And he shall not acquire many wives for himself, lest his heart turn away, nor shall he acquire for himself excessive silver and gold. (Deut. 17:16–17)

The point of those instructions—no standing army, no multiple wives, no excessive treasure—was precisely to prevent Israel's king from being one "like all the nations," one so enamored of his own glory that he turned away from dependence on God. So the witness of the book of 1 Kings against Solomon is nothing short of devastating. Read what 1 Kings has to say, and compare it to the Deuteronomy 17 passage. Solomon amassed riches:

Now the weight of gold that came to Solomon in one year was 666 talents of gold, besides that which came from the explorers and from the business of the merchants, and from all the kings of the west and from the governors of the land. King Solomon made 200 large shields of beaten gold; 600 shekels of gold went into each shield. And he made 300 shields of beaten gold; three minas of gold went into each shield. And the king put them in the House of the Forest of Lebanon. The king also made a great ivory throne and overlaid it with the finest gold. The throne had six steps, and the throne had a round top, and on each side of the seat were armrests and two lions standing beside the armrests, while twelve lions stood there, one on each end of a step on the six steps. The like of it was never made in any kingdom. All King Solomon's drinking vessels were of gold, and all the vessels of the House of the Forest of Lebanon were of pure gold. None were of silver; silver was not considered as anything in the days of Solomon. For the king had a fleet of ships of Tarshish at sea with the fleet of Hiram. Once every three years the fleet of ships of Tarshish used to come bringing gold, silver, ivory, apes, and peacocks. Thus King Solomon excelled all the kings of the earth in riches and in wisdom. (1 Kings 10:14–23)

He accumulated horses:

Solomon gathered together chariots and horsemen. He had 1,400 chariots and 12,000 horsemen. . . . And Solomon's import of horses was from Egypt. (1 Kings 10:26, 28)

And worst of all:

Now King Solomon loved many foreign women, along with the daughter of Pharaoh: Moabite, Ammonite, Edomite, Sidonian, and Hittite women, from the nations concerning which the Lord had said to the people of Israel, "You shall not enter into marriage with them, neither shall they with you, for surely they will turn away your heart after their gods." Solomon clung to these in love. He had 700 wives, who were princesses, and 300 concubines. And his wives turned away his heart. For when Solomon was old his wives turned away his heart after other gods, and his heart was not wholly true to the Lord his God, as was the heart of David his father. For Solomon went after Ashtoreth the goddess of the Sidonians, and after Milcom the abomination of the Ammonites. So Solomon did what was evil in the sight of the LORD and did not wholly follow the LORD, as David his father had done. Then Solomon built a high place for Chemosh the abomination of Moab, and for Molech the abomination of the Ammonites, on the mountain east of Jerusalem. And so he did for all his foreign wives, who made offerings and sacrificed to their gods. (1 Kings 11:1–8)

Thus Solomon broke the commands of Deuteronomy 17. His heart turned away from the Lord, and the Lord therefore declared that he would tear the kingdom out of his hand, leaving only one tribe—Judah—to be ruled by his descendants. After Solomon's death, that's precisely what happened; his son Rehoboam ascended the throne but quickly plunged the nation into civil war. The northern tribes declared their independence from the house of David, and the united Israel was torn in two—the kingdom of Israel in the north, and the kingdom of Judah in the south.

The rest of the books of Kings (and later Chronicles) tells the story of the various kings of Israel and Judah. For the most part, that story is one of compounding catastrophe as the rulers of both kingdoms descend further and further into paganism. To be sure, there were some bright spots. At least at the beginning of his reign, Asa of Judah zealously called the nation back to the worship of God alone, and Josiah too reinstituted the worship of God and worked to eradicate paganism from Judah. But overall, the story of the kings simply chronicles a long, slow shattering of the covenant with Israel. Jeroboam of Israel set up golden calf-shaped idols and called his people to worship them; his wickedness became a standard by which other kings' evil was measured. Manasseh of Judah spent most of his reign traveling the kingdom and erecting shrines to false gods. Ahaz "even burned his son as an offering, according to the despicable practices of the nations whom the LORD drove out before the people of Israel" (2 Kings 16:3), and Jehoram was so wicked that the Bible sums up his death with the stinging comment, "And he departed with no one's regret" (2 Chron. 21:20).

The rulers of the northern kingdom were, in particular, a spectacular disaster. Of the nineteen who reigned there over the course of that kingdom's two-hundred-year existence, only one (Jehu) receives even a mixed review from the authors of Kings and Chronicles, and even of him it's finally said that "he did not turn from the sins of Jeroboam the son of Nebat, which he made Israel to sin" (2 Kings 10:29). Thus in 722 BC, the northern kingdom was conquered by the armies of the king of Assyria and, according to Assyrian military policy, its inhabitants deported.

The southern kingdom of Judah persisted for a little more than another century, and during that time the prophets continued to insist that despite the wickedness of the various kings who sat on the throne of Judah, God had not abandoned his covenant with David. One day, a king would rise who would reign forever and ever, who would save his people from their sins, and who would command the honor and worship of all the nations of the earth. By 600 BC, though, those promises seemed like a fever dream. The golden age was long over, more than half the nation had been destroyed and deported by Assyria, and the rump kingdom that remained was dominated by the Babylonian Empire. In 598 BC, Nebuchadnezzar king of Babylon installed an eighteen-year-old boy by the name of Jehoiachin (or Jeconiah) as king of Judah. Three months later, though, Nebuchadnezzar apparently changed his mind, because his armies returned to Jerusalem, laid siege to it, and forced the abdication and surrender of Jehoiachin. The book of 2 Kings puts Jehoiachin's fate tersely: "And [Nebuchadnezzar] carried away Jehoiachin to Babylon" (2 Kings 24:15), presumably to die in captivity.

In Jehoiachin's place, Nebuchadnezzar installed the boy's uncle, Zedekiah, as king, but the expectation was clearly that Zedekiah would not so much rule as serve Nebuchadnezzar's own imperial interests. Ten years after his accession to the throne, Zedekiah rebelled against the king of Babylon. Nebuchadnezzar's retribution was swift and brutal. He invaded the southern kingdom yet again, though this time there was to be no mercy. Here's how 2 Kings tells the gruesome story:

> And in the ninth year of his reign, in the tenth month, on the tenth day of the month, Nebuchadnezzar king of Babylon came with all his army against Jerusalem and laid siege to it. And they built siegeworks all around it. So the city was besieged till the eleventh year of King Zedekiah. On the ninth day of the fourth month the famine was so severe in the city that there was no food for the people of the land. Then a breach was made in the city, and all the men of war fled by night by the way of the gate between the two walls, by the king's garden, and the Chaldeans were around the city. And they went in the direction of the Arabah. But the army of the Chaldeans pursued the king and overtook him in the plains of Jericho, and all his army was scattered from him. Then they captured the king and brought him up to the king of Babylon at Riblah, and they passed sentence on him. They slaughtered the sons of Zedekiah before his eyes, and put out

the eyes of Zedekiah and bound him in chains and took him to Babylon. (2 Kings 25:1–7)

The devastation for the southern kingdom was total. The armies of Babylon broke down the walls of Jerusalem and set fire to both the temple of the Lord and the palace of the king. Virtually the entire citizenry was deported to Babylon, and the city's riches were looted until nothing remained.

We talked in the last chapter about the catastrophe this represented for the people of Israel. If the Davidic line was cut off, chopped down, and left like a burned stump in the forest, then what had become of God's promise to David that his dynasty would never lack a man to sit on the throne? What had become of his promise to Abraham that one of his offspring, the one to whom the scepter belongs, would bring universal blessing to the world? What had become of the promise of Genesis 3:15 that another king would one day come to crush the serpent and save the world from the curse of death? What had become of those promises? Nothing had come of them, that's what. At least, to the tear-filled eyes of the Israelites being taken away in chains from their burning capital, that's precisely what those promises had come to—nothing but smoking wreckage. Zedekiah, the last king of Israel, would die ignominiously in Babylon, the memory of his sons' executions still seared in his mind.

The dynastic line of David was dead.

Or was it?

The last few chapters of the book of Jeremiah are dedicated to recounting the fall of Jerusalem and the total victory of Nebuchadnezzar. The sense of tragedy and despair is palpable, its last chapter chronicling the death of Zedekiah and his heirs, a listing of all that was looted from the temple before it was burned, and an accounting of the thousands of people who were taken into exile. But then . . . Jeremiah gives us these last few verses:

> In the thirty-seventh year of the exile of Jehoiachin king of Judah, in the twelfth month, on the twenty-fifth day of the month, Evil-merodach king of Babylon, in the year that he began to reign, graciously freed Jehoiachin king of Judah and brought him out of prison. And he spoke kindly to him and gave him a seat above the seats of the kings who were with him in Babylon. So Jehoiachin put off his prison garments. And every day of his life he dined regularly at the king's table, and for his allowance, a regular allowance was given him by the king, according to his daily needs, until the day of his death, as long as he lived. (Jer. 52:31–34)

In the midst of the despair and desolation, these verses crack like a thunderbolt in the darkness. King Jehoiachin, who was taken away to Babylon and presumed to have died there, is alive! Do you see the cosmic importance of this? It means that the line of David is not cut off entirely; yes it's cut down to a stump but, just as the prophets foretold, this frail old man who's been languishing in prison for thirty-seven years represents a shoot of hope, however thin, springing out of it. The royal line of David, and therefore the promises of God, are alive!

The Long-Awaited King

The New Testament begins with a genealogy—a family tree—that traces the patriarchal and royal line of Israel from Abraham through David and on down to Jesus the Christ. There are many extraordinary things about that genealogy, including this entry: "And after the deportation to Babylon: Jechoniah was the father of Shealtiel, and Shealtiel the father of Zerubbabel" (Matt. 1:12). You see? There he is—Jechoniah the exiled king (remember, Jehoiachin was also called Jechoniah), the last shoot of the dynasty of David. From him, generations later, came Jesus the Christ.

Matthew and the other Gospel writers fairly scream throughout their pages, "This one right here—this Jesus—is the long-awaited and promised King! He's the fulfillment of the promises, the one who sits on the throne of David forever, the one who will win forgiveness and salvation!" Matthew calls him "Christ" and recounts pagan kings coming from the East to worship him and offer him royal gifts. Mark tells of Jesus proclaiming that, finally, "The kingdom of God has come near!" (see Mark 1:15). And Luke records what the angel said to Jesus's mother, Mary:

> Do not be afraid, Mary, for you have found favor with God. And behold, you will conceive in your womb and bear a son, and you shall call his name Jesus. He will be great and will be called the Son of the Most High. And the Lord God will give to him the throne of his father David, and he will reign over the house of Jacob forever, and of his kingdom there will be no end. (Luke 1:30–33)

Jesus's baptism in the Jordan River by John the Baptist, at the very outset of Jesus's public ministry, is one of the most poignant moments in the New Testament history of his life—and without a doubt one of the highest peaks in the story of the biblical theme of kingship. As he comes up out of the water, a voice from heaven rings out: "This is my beloved Son, with whom I am well pleased" (Matt. 3:17). That sentence may sound straightforward, but it is packed with meaning. We'll talk about the second part of the sentence in the next chapter, but for now, it's enough to see how the theme of kingship is being moved forward with the words "This is my beloved Son." That phrase has at least two meanings. First, it is God the Father's announcement that Jesus is his dearly loved Son, the one who, as the apostle John put it later, is God's one-and-only begotten Son, the one who was with God and who in fact *was* God from the very beginning. But second, it is God's declaration that Jesus was in fact the long-awaited Messiah, the King of Israel. It was Israel herself whom God first called "my son" when he brought her out of Egypt (Ex. 4:22), but later the title was given to the king, who represented the entire nation before God (2 Sam. 7:14; Ps. 2:12). Here, Jesus is given that title; he steps into the office of the Davidic King of Israel. Having stood unoccupied for six hundred years, the throne of Israel was no longer empty.

Mark records that after Jesus's baptism, "The Spirit immediately drove him out into the wilderness" (Mark 1:12), and there he confronted the great enemy of mankind—the serpent, the dragon, Satan. Do you see the significance of what's happening there? Jesus, having stepped into the role and office of king, immediately begins to do what the king was supposed to do all along—fight his people's enemies and win battles for them that they could not win for themselves. So he confronts the foe from the garden, endures his temptations, and—for the first time—defeats him. King Jesus was beginning to do what King Adam,

King David, or any other king of Israel never could—crush the head of the serpent.

Throughout the course of his ministry, the nature of Jesus's kingship became clearer and clearer. To be sure, most people, including his own disciples, misunderstood it entirely. So once Jesus proved he could essentially make food out of nothing, the people tried to seize him and make him king by force (John 6:15)! There was certainly some logic in it; in a fight against the Romans, never having to worry about food for the army would have been a significant advantage! The leaders of the people were equally convinced that Jesus was a political revolutionary, but to them, his claims to kingship were sufficient reason to turn him over to the Romans. Pressed by the Roman governor Pontius Pilate, though, Jesus made clear that his kingship was not the kind anyone expected: "My kingdom is not of this world. If my kingdom were of this world, my servants would have been fighting, that I might not be delivered over to the Jews. But my kingdom is not from the world" (John 18:36). The most striking reflection of the unique nature of Jesus's kingship was the scene on Golgotha on the Friday when Jesus was crucified: a beaten, dying man wearing a crown fashioned out of thorns, a handwritten sign hanging over his head that read "Jesus of Nazareth, the King of the Jews." The sign, though it intended to mock, spoke better than it knew. Jesus was not just any king, but a crucified King who died in the place of his people. The interplay between the biblical themes of kingship and sacrifice are deep and rich, and we'll explore them at length in the next chapter.

After Jesus's resurrection, the throne and crown of David were universalized. "All authority," Jesus declared, "in heaven and on earth has been given to me" (Matt. 28:18). This was a world-changing proclamation. No longer was the king of Israel the ruler of a small, relatively insignificant country on the world stage; now, just as the prophets had said, the Davidic King would rule over all, and the rulers of the nations would come to pay him homage.

The main aim of the book of Revelation is to encourage the beleaguered churches of Jesus to remain firm and hold fast to the faith. The world is not out of control, the book proclaims. King Jesus is on the throne, ruling and reigning for the good of his church, and someday soon he will return to rescue his people and rule over a new heavens and new earth. One of the last and most striking visions in the book of Revelation is of Jesus finally, once and for all, destroying the serpent:

> Then I saw an angel coming down from heaven, holding in his hand the key to the bottomless pit and a great chain. And he seized the dragon, that ancient serpent, who is the devil and Satan, and bound him for a thousand years, and threw him into the pit, and shut it and sealed it over him, so that he might not deceive the nations any longer, until the thousand years were ended. . . . And when the thousand years are ended, Satan will be released from his prison and will come out to deceive the nations that are at the four corners of the earth, Gog and Magog, to gather them for battle; their number is like the sand of the sea. And they marched up over the broad plain of the earth and surrounded the camp of the saints and the beloved city, but fire came down from heaven and consumed them, and the devil who had deceived them was thrown into the lake of fire and sulfur where the beast and the false prophet were, and

they will be tormented day and night forever and ever. (Rev. 20:1–3, 7–10; see also Matt. 12:29 and Mark 3:27)

So King Jesus the Resurrected finally accomplishes what King Adam the Fallen had failed so miserably to do. He reigns over the entire creation, bringing all things into submission to himself (Eph. 1:22; Heb. 2:8) and ultimately to God (1 Cor. 15:24), and he fulfills—finally—the promise of Genesis 3:15 by destroying the serpent once and for all.

6

Without Blood, There Is No Forgiveness

The Theme of Sacrifice

LET ME START this chapter with a question (with some setup first). Throughout Christian history, Christians have always affirmed that Jesus holds a threefold office on behalf of his people. He is, at once, their Prophet, Priest, and King. Knowing that, with which one of those offices do you normally associate his death on the cross? In my experience, most Christians would answer "Priest." And that's a good answer. After all, Jesus's death on the cross was ultimately a *sacrifice*—a substitutionary death in the place of and on behalf of another—and therefore it's natural to associate it with Jesus's priestly office. In fact, the book of Hebrews makes the point explicitly that when Jesus died for his people, he was acting as the great high priest who was making a final, once-for-all sacrifice to save his people from their sins.

And yet, all four Gospel narratives of Jesus's death are shot through not so much with priestly imagery but with *kingly* imagery. As Jesus is scourged by the Romans, he's dressed in imperial purple, given a reed to act as a scepter, and coronated with a bunch of thorns fashioned into a crown. As he hangs dying, nailed to the cross, the Roman governor orders a sign to be hung over his head reading "Jesus of Nazareth, the King of the Jews." The point of all this is that the Gospel narratives seem to be fairly screaming to us that, in some beautifully and yet wrenchingly ironic way, Jesus is dying not just as Priest but *as King*—that his death is somehow particularly and uniquely *kinglike work*. This strikes us as a strange idea. Suffering and death are not things we usually associate with kingship. Kings are about power and ruling. When we want to talk about Jesus's sovereignty and majesty, we call him King of kings. But when we want to talk about his suffering and humiliation, we tend to reach for priestly language.

But here's what I want you to see as we trace the biblical theme of sacrifice in this chapter. Jesus's death in his people's place, his salvation of them from their sins, is naturally and rightly and inherently tied to his office as King. In fact, you can't understand kingship without understanding that. You can't rightly proclaim Jesus as King without proclaiming him also as suffering Savior. Indeed, the whole epic story of the Bible strains toward the good news that God's people will be saved not just by a King, but by the blood of a slaughtered King.

We'll get to all that shortly, but first some stage setting. This chapter traces the biblical theme of *sacrifice*, which is a critical and well-known strand of the Bible's storyline. I'd venture to say that, generally speaking, if people know anything about the Old

Testament, they know that it involved—one way or another—sacrifices of animals to deal with, to atone for, people's sins before God. The idea of sacrifice has come in for hard treatment by non-Christian and non-Jewish scholars through the centuries, but when you come right down to it, the fact is undeniable: the reality and theology of sacrifice is critically important to the unfolding of the epic story of the Bible. In fact, the whole thing becomes incoherent without it.

Why is that? Well, if you've been reading this book carefully, then you've probably noticed that in every one of the themes we've traced so far—God's presence with his people, God's covenants with his people, God's kingship over his people—one piece of the puzzle has been conspicuously missing: Exactly *how* does each of those themes get from the cataclysm of the fall to the glory of salvation? Think about it. We know that the Bible says that God works to be present again with his people, but how exactly does that happen after they have so high-handedly rebelled against him? We've seen that God makes a new covenant with his people, but exactly how can that come to pass once the first covenants have been shattered by his people's sin? And how, exactly, can he be king over them when they have so decisively rejected his authority and his crown? Do all these remarkable changes happen just by divine *fiat*? Does he just declare, by sheer force of will, "So it shall be?" No, the answer to all these questions is, "He does it through sacrifice." Another great engine that drives all the themes of the epic story of the Bible from fall to glory is sacrifice.

Unlike the other themes we've traced in this book, the theme of sacrifice begins only after the fall of Adam and Eve into sin. It would have been unnecessary prior to that. Not only so, but its beginning is relatively modest, just a kind of aside in the fallout of Adam's rebellion against God. The story goes like this: Once they have disobeyed God and eaten the fruit of the tree of the knowledge of good and evil, Adam and Eve's innocence is stripped away and they become aware of their nakedness before God— their exposed shame before the divine eyes. They initially clothed themselves in fig leaves, but the theme of sacrifice is launched in one particular detail in Genesis 3:21: "And the LORD God made for Adam and for his wife garments of skins and clothed them." On a first reading, that sentence seems entirely unremarkable, but it is actually a poignant, if cloudy, beginning to the theme of sacrifice that will stretch throughout the rest of the Bible. After all, there can be no skins for clothing unless an animal died. Adam and Eve's nakedness—their shame, their raw exposure before the judgment of God—was covered only when some other creature gave its life for that purpose.

The death of those animals, whatever they were, raises the question of the penalty for sin in the first place. God was clear when he gave instructions to Adam not to eat the fruit of the tree in the middle of the garden: "Of the tree of the knowledge of good and evil you shall not eat, for in the day that you eat of it *you shall surely die*" (Gen. 2:17). But why the penalty of death and not something else? Why couldn't God have declared, "In the day that you eat of it you shall surely get very sick," or something else? Why death? The answer lies in what we've already discovered about the true nature of Adam's sin. In eating the fruit, he wasn't simply violating some minor rule handed down by heaven; he was declaring war against and independence from the God who had created him. Not only that, he was declaring independence from the God who sustained him in life. That's the reason why death was the only right and fitting punishment for Adam's sin: when you declare independence from the very source of your life, it shouldn't be super surprising when death is what results.

Through Genesis 4–5, the penalty of death tightens its hellish grip on humanity. The first son of Adam and Eve, Cain, murders his younger brother. Chapter 5 then consists of a genealogy of Adam's descendants down to Noah, each entry ending with an iron refrain: "and he died," "and he died," "and he died." But then there's Enoch in 5:21–24. Enoch's entry in the genealogy doesn't end with his death, but rather with "Enoch walked with God, and he was not, for God took him" (Gen. 5:24). It's a surprising departure from the norm, but the point is clear enough. It is as if God were saying, "The drumbeat of death's iron grip on humanity is strong, yes. But I can arrest it, I can *stop it*, anytime I want. Death will not have the last word."

After Genesis 5 and the story of Noah and the flood, the Bible's story focuses for a long time on Abraham—on the cutting of God's covenant with him and the provision of a son, Isaac, who would be the necessary first step in God's making Abraham's descendants into "a great nation." There are twists and turns and ups and downs, but the first words of Genesis 22 are nothing short of shocking, if not appalling: "After these things God tested Abraham and said to him, 'Abraham!' And he said, 'Here I am.' He said, 'Take your son, your only son Isaac, whom you love, and go to the land of Moriah, and offer him there as a burnt offering on one of the mountains of which I shall tell you'" (Gen. 22:1–2).

Sacrifice Isaac! The demand was preposterous, more than Abraham should have been able to bear, and for more than one reason.

For one thing, there's the very idea of *human* sacrifice. It was the pagan gods—Chemosh, Molech, Baal—who demanded human sacrifice, not the God of Israel. And yet here was the Lord demanding just that. More, the death of Isaac would have meant the death of God's promises. After all, Isaac was the promised means by which Abraham would be made a great nation, and therefore he was also the means by which the promised offspring would be born to bring blessing to the nations of the Lord. If Isaac died, none of that could happen. Consequently, God's demand that Abraham put Isaac to death was a fundamental test of Abraham's faith. God had promised; could God now deliver, even through *this*?

Through the centuries, God's command to Abraham that he should sacrifice his son Isaac has drawn no end of objection and vitriol. That's not surprising. It's a shocking command, one fitting perhaps for the pagan gods of the Canaanite nations who lived in the land at the time, but surely not for the God of the Bible. Here, some more understanding of the situation is helpful. For one thing, God has the absolute right to take any life he chooses. Since the fall, every human being—including Isaac—lives under a commuted sentence of death. Every one of us lives another minute only by the grace of God, and not one of us would be the victim of injustice if God were to demand our lives this very minute. So it was with Isaac; God had every right to demand that the commuted sentence of death be executed immediately. In fact, the Lord made this principle clear to his people in a particular way in the aftermath of the exodus from Egypt:

The Lord said to Moses, "Consecrate to me all the firstborn. Whatever is the first to open the womb among the people of

Israel, both of man and of beast, is mine. . . . All the firstborn of your animals that are males shall be the LORD's. Every firstborn of a donkey you shall redeem with a lamb, or if you will not redeem it you shall break its neck. Every firstborn of man among your sons you shall redeem. (Ex. 13:1–2, 12–13)

God gave these instructions in the aftermath of the Passover, when he had spared the firstborn of Israel but allowed the destroyer to kill all the firstborn of Egypt. The result of that, God says, is that all the firstborn of Israel belong to him; they are consecrated to him. For an animal like a donkey, for example, an Israelite had a choice of how to surrender that animal to God— he could either kill it or offer another animal in its place to redeem it. For a human firstborn child, the principle was the same—that child was consecrated to God—but the Israelite didn't have a choice like he did for an animal. He *had* to redeem his child by offering another animal to die in the child's place.

The striking thing is that Abraham seemed to be well aware of the general principle underlying even those later commands: God gives human life, and because all humans live under a sentence of death, he can demand that life anytime he wishes. So Abraham takes Isaac to the mountain. What happens next is bated-breath-level dramatic:

When they came to the place of which God had told him, Abraham built the altar there and laid the wood in order and bound Isaac his son and laid him on the altar, on top of the wood. Then Abraham reached out his hand and took the knife to slaughter his son. But the angel of the LORD called to him from heaven and said, "Abraham, Abraham!" And he said, "Here I am." He said, "Do not lay your hand on the boy or do anything to him, for now I know that you fear God, seeing you have not withheld your son, your only son, from me." And Abraham lifted up his eyes and looked, and behold, behind him was a ram, caught in a thicket by his horns. And Abraham went and took the ram and offered it up as a burnt offering instead of his son. (Gen. 22:9–13)

Clearly, Abraham fully expected for God *not* to stop the knife from plunging into Isaac's heart. He raised the knife and was about to let it fall before God called out to him to stop. And why wouldn't Abraham have thought that? After all, every one of the other pagan gods of the nations around him demanded human sacrifice. Molech did, Chemosh did, Baal did—all of them. So why would *this* God be any different? But that's at least one of the points God was making to Abraham in the most dramatic way possible—that he *wasn't* like those other gods, not in the least. Though he had every right to demand the execution of the death sentence on every sinner, the God of Abraham was declaring that he would not do that. Instead, he would allow *another* to die in the sinner's place, in this case a ram caught in a thicket, which Abraham offered "instead of his son." Most Christians, when they read the story of Abraham almost sacrificing Isaac, tend to put themselves in the place of Abraham: "Would I obey God under similar circumstances? Would I be able to offer to God that which is most dear to me?" But that's not the point of the story, not most profoundly. Most importantly, we as readers are not in the place of Abraham so much as we are in the place of Isaac—doomed to die, about to be executed, and yet rescued in the nick of time by one who dies in our place.

In the book of Exodus, God continues to teach his people about the nature of sacrifice. This was especially true on the night of Passover. Prior to that night, God told his people that he was going to send the destroyer through all the land of Egypt—including the lands the Israelites themselves inhabited—to kill the firstborn of every family. This would happen to the Israelites as well as the Egyptians unless they followed God's very specific instructions:

> Tell all the congregation of Israel that on the tenth day of this month every man shall take a lamb according to their fathers' houses, a lamb for a household. . . . Your lamb shall be without blemish, a male a year old. You may take it from the sheep or from the goats, and you shall keep it until the fourteenth day of this month, when the whole assembly of the congregation of Israel shall kill their lambs at twilight.
>
> Then they shall take some of the blood and put it on the two doorposts and the lintel of the houses in which they eat it. They shall eat the flesh that night, roasted on the fire; with unleavened bread and bitter herbs they shall eat it. . . . For I will pass through the land of Egypt that night, and I will strike all the firstborn in the land of Egypt, both man and beast; and on all the gods of Egypt I will execute judgments: I am the LORD. The blood shall be a sign for you, on the houses where you are. And when I see the blood, I will pass over you, and no plague will befall you to destroy you, when I strike the land of Egypt. (Ex. 12:3–13)

The "Passover," as it was aptly called, became one of the highest holy days of the Jewish year, and it's not hard to see why. The Lord was teaching his people about sacrifice. As each family chose a lamb out of their flock, slaughtered it, and smeared the blood on their doorframe, they all would know that this lamb had died in the place of their own firstborn child. The child had been saved—redeemed—by the blood of the lamb.

Through the years, the Lord continued to teach his people about the meaning of sacrifice. In Exodus 17, though, he pushed the theme forward dramatically, intimating that in the end, it wouldn't be an animal who would die in the place of sinners, but someone else. Here's the story as it's told in the book of Exodus:

> All the congregation of the people of Israel moved on from the wilderness of Sin by stages, according to the commandment of the LORD, and camped at Rephidim, but there was no water for the people to drink. Therefore the people quarreled with Moses and said, "Give us water to drink." And Moses said to them, "Why do you quarrel with me? Why do you test the LORD?" But the people thirsted there for water, and the people grumbled against Moses and said, "Why did you bring us up out of Egypt, to kill us and our children and our livestock with thirst?" So Moses cried to the LORD, "What shall I do with this people? They are almost ready to stone me." And the LORD said to Moses, "Pass on before the people, taking with you some of the elders of Israel, and take in your hand the staff with which you struck the Nile, and go. Behold, I will stand before you there on the rock at Horeb, and you shall strike the rock, and water shall come out of it, and the people

will drink." And Moses did so, in the sight of the elders of Israel. (Ex. 17:1–6)

The situation was dire. Israel was out of water, and blaming God for their plight. More, they were essentially charging God with murder, which Moses makes clear when he says they want to stone him. They couldn't get the rocks high enough to hit God, so they would stone God's spokesman instead. God calls their bluff, basically telling Moses to declare that a formal trial is about to be held. The elders of the people are marched in like judges, and Moses's staff is brought too. The presence of that staff is an ominous development, because everyone knew it was a staff of judgment, a staff of death. This was the staff Moses held out over the Nile when it turned to blood and over the Red Sea when it crashed down on the Egyptian army. The message of that staff was, "Someone is about to be found guilty; someone is about to be struck with this rod and die." But who? Was God the guilty one? No! It was, emphatically, the people of Israel who were guilty. God had been unfailingly and extravagantly gracious to them— rescuing them from slavery, providing sustenance in the desert, protecting them from Pharaoh's armies. And at every turn, in the face of every gracious divine action, the Israelites had grumbled and complained. They were ungrateful, sinful rebels, and the rod of judgment was about to fall on *them*. But then this happens:

And the Lord said to Moses, "Pass on before the people, taking with you some of the elders of Israel, and take in your hand the staff with which you struck the Nile, and go. Behold, I will stand before you there on the rock at Horeb, and you shall strike the rock, and water shall come out of it, and the people will drink." And Moses did so. (Ex. 17:5–6)

It's an easy detail to miss, but a critical one: When Moses's staff of judgment fell on the rock, *where was God?* According to verse 6, he was there—"on the rock." You see the point? The judgment which by every right should have fallen on the people of Israel *fell on God instead.* And the result was that water—life!—poured forth. This was a momentous advance of the biblical theme of sacrifice. God was showing his people not just that it did not have to be the sinner who died for his own sin, but that ultimately it would be God himself who would suffer that ultimate punishment for his people. How exactly that would happen was still unclear and cloudy, but it would become clearer in centuries to come.

In the latter half of Exodus and through the book of Leviticus, God instituted a complicated and deeply meaningful system of sacrifices for his people. In fact, there were five main types of sacrifice. There was the grain offering by which Israelites could declare their commitment to their heavenly King. The peace offering was a celebration of God's grace capped by a grand feast with the sacrificer's friends and family. The sin offering cleansed the tabernacle for ceremonial use. The guilt offering seems to have been the restitution required when someone sinned particularly against the temple or the priests. And then there was the main offering—the burnt offering—which was the main sacrifice for sins, the one offered by individual families and then once a year by the nation as a whole on the Day of Atonement.

All these sacrifices provided structure and rhythm to the daily, weekly, and yearly lives of the Israelites. Indeed, the prophets often had to remind the people that what ultimately mattered was not the burning of an animal but rather the worshiper's heart of commitment to God. But as the story of the Bible unfolds, what is most striking is how the theme of sacrifice begins to wrap more and more tightly together with kingship. In the end, in fact, it becomes clear that the final, greatest sacrifice will be offered *by Israel's king.* Indeed, that becomes the principle task and nature of kingship in Israel—to represent the people and to suffer in their place.

When David arrives on the scene in 1 Samuel, the story's focus is not only on the bare events that led David to the throne, but also (as we said in the last chapter) on the role and responsibility of Israel's king. And what is that role and responsibility? It is particularly *representation* and *suffering*—that is, to represent the people and therefore to suffer for them. As the story plays out, it becomes clear that *this is what the king does.* He represents the people in himself, and he *suffers.* Let's think for a moment about both.

A Representative King

The role of representation is not a terribly hard concept to grasp. Sovereigns are often said to represent the very identity of the nation they rule. That idea of the sovereign symbolically *being* the nation was a strong theme in the Israelite idea of kingship. Consider, for example, the title "Son of God." Most Christians are familiar with that phrase mainly as a title for Jesus; it refers to his identity as the second person of the Trinity, the ontological *Son* of God the Father. But in the story of the Bible, the phrase "Son of God" had another meaning as well—it was a well-known throne-title for the king of Israel. So in 2 Samuel 7, God declared to David about his royal descendants, "I will be to him a father, and he shall be to me a son" (7:14). In Psalm 2, David writes about the king of Israel, "The LORD said to me, 'You are my Son'" (2:7). In Psalm 89 God says of the king,

> He shall cry to me, "You are my Father,
>   my God, and the Rock of my salvation."
> And I will make him the firstborn,
>   the highest of the kings of the earth. (89:26–27)

That's all well and good, but why would the phrase "Son of God" have become a throne name for the king of Israel in the first place, and how is it important in understanding the role of the king as a representative of the people? The answer lies in Exodus 4:22–23 where God says to Moses, "Then you shall say to Pharaoh, 'Thus says the LORD, Israel is my firstborn son, and I say to you, "Let my son go that he may serve me."'" You see? The reason the king could be "son" and "firstborn" of God was that the entire nation of Israel *first* was "son" and "firstborn" of God. The identity of the nation was taken up and summed up in the person of the king. They were united to him. He represented them.

This royal representation is important, because it means that the king was understood to act for the nation in important ways. What he did, they did; what he did had ramifications for them. For example, in 1 Chronicles 21, Joab pleads with David not to do a census of the fighting men among the people because it would be an act of disbelief in God's ability to protect the nation. Joab says: "'Why then should my lord require this? Why should it be a cause of guilt for Israel?' But the king's word prevailed against Joab. . . . But God was displeased with this thing, and he struck Israel" (21:3–4, 7). You see? It was the king who acted sinfully and in unbelief, but it was *Israel* whom God struck in punishment. Here's the point: what happens to the king happens to the people, and what happens to the people happens to their king. The two are inseparably united to one another. He represents them, meaning that he stands in their place.

A Suffering King

There's another part to the king's role, though. Not only does the king *represent* the people, but another part of his paradigmatic role is to *suffer*. David learned that to be king is to suffer. His road to the throne is not one of royal ease; it's one of suffering. He lives in the wilderness, in caves, in enemy territory; his reign is wracked by family strife, civil war, and the consequences of sin. More, the promise of suffering for the king is explicit in the Davidic covenant: "When he commits iniquity, I will discipline him with the rod of men, with the stripes of the sons of men" (2 Sam. 7:14). And so many of the psalms are, essentially, David crying out in distress in pain, sometimes as an individual man, but especially in book two of the Psalms as *the very voice of the nation*. Indeed, by the end of book three, Psalm 89 depicts nothing but shame and despair for the king and therefore the nation itself.

Through the reign of David, the role and responsibility of the king of Israel is beginning to become clearer. But still, what we have are not much more than a few disparate, disconnected shards of meaning. The king would represent. And the king would suffer. But what do those have to do with each other, and how do they lead to salvation? To be sure, Israel had an understanding already of vicarious suffering, of sacrifice—one *thing* suffering for another, dying so that another wouldn't have to. We've seen that in the first part of this chapter. But what does that kind of thing have to do with the king? It's not at all clear. Sacrifice, representation, suffering, the kingship—all lying there like the shards of Narsil. What do they mean? And what do they become when you put them together? The answer to those questions would begin to come clear as the prophets revealed more of God's plan and purpose.

Representation by Sacrifice

By the end of David's life, it was abundantly clear that he wasn't the one who was finally going to bring salvation to the world. In his wake, the kingdom split, Assyria invaded the north, and king after king proved to be colossal failures to meet God's standard for kingship in Israel. Through all these centuries, though—at least four of them—the prophets picked up these threads of kingship, union, representation, and suffering, and began to weave them together into a breathtaking picture of a King who would represent his people *by suffering for them*, and so save them from their sins. Let's look at two places in the prophets where this picture is forged.

The book of Isaiah is composed of three smaller books that combine into one brilliant prophetic message. The first might best be called the book of the king. In it God reaffirms his determination, even in the wake of Uzziah's awful death, to keep the now-piled-up promises of Genesis 3, Numbers 24, 2 Samuel 7, and Psalm 2 to send a Messianic King to set all things right.

But then there's the second part of Isaiah, which we might call the book of the suffering servant. This second book describes a person, the servant of the Lord, who suffers in the place of his people as a sacrifice for their sins. But the shocker is that as you read Isaiah, you realize that this promised King and this suffering servant *are one and the same person.* You see? The shards are coming together. Through the book of Isaiah, you can start to see how the king's representation of the people and the king's suffering fit together. God's promises to save his people would be fulfilled by a King who would not just suffer but would suffer *as the representative sacrifice in the place of his people*—for them, in their place.

The book of Zechariah makes the same point, but with a dramatic image. The book focuses on the two main offices in Israel—priest and king. To understand its message, though, you have to understand that since the fall in Eden, those two offices had been kept complementary but, with few exceptions, strictly separate. In fact, in large part it was forbidden for the king to perform the duties of a priest. When King Uzziah tried, God struck him with leprosy, and he died outside the city of Jerusalem in a village of lepers. So at the outset, Zechariah says—quite unsurprisingly at first—that God intends to save his people through those two offices, the priest and the king. The prophetic vision of Zechariah 3 introduces Joshua the high priest, and the vision of Zechariah 4 introduces Zerubbabel the governor (the closest thing Israel had to a king in the years following their return to Jerusalem). But then something astonishing happens: "And the word of the LORD came to me: 'Take from the exiles . . . who have arrived from Babylon. . . . Take from them silver and gold, and make crowns, and set it on the head of Joshua . . . the high priest" (Zech. 6:9–11).[1]

Two details in those verses are intended to capture your attention as a reader. For one thing, notice that Zechariah is initially told to take the silver and gold and make *crowns*, plural—two of them. But then he's told to take *it*—singular, *one* crown—and set it on somebody's head. Whose head? That's the second thing: Zechariah is told to crown not Zerubbabel the governor, but Joshua the high priest. Given the separation between king and priest, the crowning of Joshua is an absolutely stunning development, so much in fact that some scholars have insisted that Zechariah must have gotten the name wrong and it really was Zerubbabel who was crowned. But actually, that's the whole point! The crowning of Joshua is an acted-out parable to show that one day, kingship and priesthood would be merged together—two crowns forged into one. No longer would there be a priest who would atone and perform sacrifices for sin *and* a king who would rule and represent and suffer. Instead, there would be a single, united priest-king who would represent the people *by* offering himself as a sacrifice for them.

Zechariah ends his book by driving all of this home, prophesying that the people of Israel ultimately would reject their King, pierce him, and run him through—and that, gloriously, salvation and redemption will result from his death. Just as water flowed

---

1 This is my own translation of the Hebrew. The ESV translates it as "make a crown, and set it on the head of Joshua," smoothing out the strange grammar created by "crowns" (plural) and "set it" (singular). The NASB and NIV do the same thing, keeping the singular throughout. KJV and HCSB both go the other direction, making all the words plural—"make crowns, and set them." But the underlying Hebrew uses both singular and plural words—"make *crowns*, and set *it* on the head of Joshua." Yes, it's bad grammar, but it's very deliberate. Read on to find out why.

from the stricken rock on which God stood, just as life resulted from the spilled blood of the Passover lamb, so the death of the King would bring salvation. Ultimately, that's what being king meant; this is what the king does. He stands in the place of his people to absorb the wrath that should have fallen on them.

Of course all of this comes to its ultimate end and goal and fulfillment when the angel says to Joseph about his fiancée, Mary, "She will bear a son, and you shall call his name Jesus, for he will save his people from their sins" (Matt. 1:21). By the beginning of his ministry, Jesus was well aware that God had appointed him King of Israel, and he also knew what being king meant. To take the crown, to be the king, was also to be the suffering servant who would die to save his people. So he said in Mark 10:45 that he had come to "give his life as a ransom for many," and in John 10:11 that he would "lay down his life for the sheep," and ultimately in Matthew 26:28 that his blood was about to be "poured out for many for the forgiveness of sins."

Even at his baptism, Jesus was marked out as the King who would die for his people. We saw in the last chapter how the words "This is my beloved Son" marked Jesus as the eternal Son of God *and* as the King of Israel (Matt. 3:17). But that second phrase—"with whom I am well-pleased"—is certainly God's honest opinion of his Son, but it is also a quotation of Isaiah 42:1, which introduces the suffering servant of the Lord. Thus with those few words from heaven, God was setting on Jesus's head the triple crown—the crown of heaven as God's Son, the crown of Israel as the long-awaited Messiah, and the crown of thorns as the suffering servant who would save his people by representing them and finally dying in their place.

It's wonderful, isn't it, how all of these themes that make up the epic story of the Bible—God's presence, God's covenants, the kingship, and sacrifice—all weave together in various ways until they come to rest on the crowned head of Jesus Christ! You can see how it all comes together. Through Jesus's sacrificial death on the cross and resurrection, the curtain in the temple is torn in two as people are brought back into God's presence, the new covenant is inaugurated by which God binds himself to his people once and for all, and Satan—the dragon, that serpent of old—is fully and finally defeated by the King of kings and Lord of lords.

> Crown him with many crowns,
> The Lamb upon his throne!
> Hark! how the heavenly anthem drowns
> All music but its own.
> Awake, my soul, and sing
> of him who died for thee,
> and hail him as thy matchless king
> through all eternity.[2]

---

2 Matthew Bridges, "Crown Him with Many Crowns," 1851.

7

Setting Out

BY THE END of my pre-trek briefing in Kathmandu, my mind was full of information and the adrenaline was already pumping. I was ready to go—right then and there—to the mountains! I was ready to see the snowcaps, climb to elevations I'd probably never experience again, enjoy the thrill of actually laying my eyes on things I'd only read about or maybe seen in movies. But my guide wasn't quite done. He'd given us a flyover understanding of the path we'd be taking to Base Camp, he'd oriented us to the sights and points of interest we'd see, and he'd even given us a good overview of the history of Nepal, of the Khumbu Region, and even of Everest itself. But there was one more section of the briefing still left—essentially, Things That Can Kill You.

To be sure, there are a number of obvious things that can kill you in the Himalayas. You can fall off the side of a mountain, and die. You can get crushed by an avalanche, and die. There can be a freak snowstorm or a freak earthquake (there had been one of those just the year past!) or a freak broken bone, and you can die.

But besides all of those horrors, the guide warned of two other deadly dangers to watch out for. One of those was altitude sickness, a deadly serious condition that results from rapid exposure to the low oxygen levels at high altitudes. Headaches, dizziness, an appearance of drunkenness, slurred speech are the initial symptoms, but they progress quickly toward cerebral edema and death if not treated correctly. Thus, our guide told us to be hyper-vigilant about those symptoms. A headache isn't just a headache in the Himalayas, and morning grogginess isn't just your body complaining about a lack of sleep. Acute mountain sickness is a killer, and every climber and trekker has to learn to respect it.

We had to watch out for another danger as well in the mountains, less ominous-sounding perhaps than acute mountain sickness but, believe it or not, according to the statistics, almost as deadly: yaks. I kid you not; the guide warned us about yaks. Himalayan yaks aren't prone to attack or stampede or anything like it. But the trails we'd be walking on were also the main economic arteries of the Khumbu Region, and since it's impossible for automobiles to operate in the mountains, goods of every kind are often transported by yak. What this means is that at regular intervals, many times a day, trekking tourists will meet a Sherpa courier with a herd of yaks on the extremely narrow trail, and everyone then has to figure out how to get past one another. The thing is, though, yaks don't have social skills. They don't stop, they don't make room for an easy pass, they don't say "Excuse me." They just lumber on down the trail one-hundred-percent heedless of what that might mean for any trekkers in their way. Now here's the important part: When you meet a herd of them on the trail, our guides told us, *you absolutely must stay on the mountain side of the yaks!* Why mountain side? Because anytime you catch a solid booty-bump from a half-ton yak, you're going to go somewhere—fast and with much momentum! And, for obvious reasons, it's far better to get yak-whacked *into* the side of the mountain than *off* the side of the mountain!

You laugh, but people have died from carelessly standing on the wrong side of a hip-swaying yak!

Now, in all likelihood, reading the Bible's epic story from start to finish isn't going to put you in danger of developing acute mountain sickness or getting knocked off a mountain by an inconsiderate beast of burden. Still, though, there are dangers to be aware of as you read, mistakes and errors that people often make that lead them to misunderstand the Bible and therefore misunderstand God, Jesus Christ, and even themselves as human beings. So in this chapter, I want to make you aware of a handful of those errors so you can be on the lookout for them and—so to speak—stay mountainside of them. Finally, I want to give you some words of advice and encouragement before you set out. But first, let me flag four dangers for you.

First, don't go it alone. One of the worst and first mistakes people often make when they set out to read the Bible is deciding they're going to do so with "just me, my God, and my Bible." You can certainly do that, and you'll certainly benefit from reading the Bible that way. But you won't benefit as much as when you read it with other people—people you can share insights and questions with, or people who have read and studied it more than you. The Bible is a rich and deeply layered story, and your reading of it will be enriched by having someone who can say things like, "Look at this" or "Did you see that?" or "Remember that, because it's going to be important later!" This is why the Lord put Christians together in churches—so we could read and respond to his word together and grow up into Christian maturity together, rather than just as individuals. If you want to experience the greatest, highest treasures that the story of the Bible contains, you'll unite yourself to a local church where you can explore it all with other Christians.

Second, as you read the Bible's story, never forget that it's a story. It moves, it develops, things change, and surprises await. The Bible is a not a static manual for life, as if every page of it is to be understood in exactly the same way. For example, the covenant with Israel literally shaped the life of an entire nation for centuries; entire books of the Bible explain its heart, its meaning, its stipulations, and its rules. And yet by the end of the story, the author of Hebrews will call that covenant "obsolete" (Heb. 8:13). Christians can—and have and will continue to—debate exactly what that means, but obviously *something* has changed. The story has progressed. So when somebody dives into Leviticus and says, "So why do you Christians wear mixed-fabric clothing, and why are you okay eating lobsters?" they're misunderstanding the nature of a story. Imagine reading the first chapter of *The Hobbit*, hearing Bilbo say "I have no use for adventures. Nasty, disturbing, and uncomfortable things. Make you late for dinner!" and then insisting that the rest of the book is a *contradiction* of that line. It's not a contradiction; it's a story! And part of the magnificence of the story is that Bilbo can go from saying *that* to slaying a dragon.

Many, many similar things happen as the themes of the biblical story unfold. God tells his people to perform sacrifices, then declares those to be no more in the wake of the ultimate sacrifice of his Son. He gives the Israelites food laws—what they can eat and what they can't—but then Mark says of Jesus, "Thus he declared all foods clean" (Mark 7:19). Those aren't contradictions; they're not God being wishy-washy or changing his mind. They are movements, developments, plot points in a swelling, rolling, moving narrative. Don't forget that the Bible is a story.

Third, don't panic when you run into things in the Bible that you don't understand, or that don't make sense to you at first. That's to be expected in a story as sweeping and complex—and as varied in genre—as the biblical epic. Regardless of what the problem is, don't panic and assume that there's no good answer to it. The fact is, Christians have been thinking about—and critics have been firing at—the Bible for over 2,000 years. Whatever question you have, I promise that there are good answers to it. You just have to find the right person to ask or the right book to consult. In fact, it's precisely at those points where you think there's a problem—where Jesus seems to dodge a question, for instance, or where two crowns are forged but then *"it"* is set on the high priest's head—where you find the most magnificent treasures. Don't jump to the conclusion and think, "These were primitive people writing this book, so they must have misspoken." Instead, trust that the one great author behind the epic story knew what he was doing, and there are treasures to be found even in—usually *especially* in—the places that at first trip you up.

Fourth, from start to finish, never lose sight of the goal of the whole story—Jesus Christ. After his resurrection, Jesus surprised a couple of his followers as they were walking along the road to the town of Emmaus, near Jerusalem. In the conversation that followed, Luke tells us that Jesus gave those followers a crash course in the real meaning of the Old Testament: "And beginning with Moses and all the Prophets, he interpreted to them in all the Scriptures the things concerning himself" (Luke 24:27). In other words, he taught them to see the goal and end of the story—himself. If you keep that in mind—that all the themes of the Bible finally come to their fulfillment in Jesus—you'll be a much more astute reader of the Bible. You won't get lost on rabbit trails; you won't find yourself missing the point of passages (like so many do, for example with David and Goliath or Abraham's offering of Isaac); you won't overemphasize something that isn't actually important. Instead, keeping your eyes firmly on Jesus, you'll begin to see how the whole grand narrative elegantly and beautifully swirls together until it spotlights *him* in a hundred different colors.

With all that said, and all of those dangers highlighted now, let me encourage you with some final words before you begin this great journey. First, *have fun* reading the Bible! So many Christians read the Bible as if it's mainly a duty, or hard work. They read it for daily devotions because they think they have to, or they read it thinking they have to "get something out of it for daily living" or be "convicted" by something in it. To be sure, all that has its place, but have you ever read the Bible just for fun? Just for the sheer joy of letting the movie play in your imagination, of seeing—in your own mind—the look on Moses's face when the Red Sea splits, or of hearing the gasps from the army when the walls of Jericho flattened as if a bomb went off in the center of the city? The biblical story is a wild, wild ride, and there's a place for reading it simply for the sheer joy of it.

Here's another piece of advice: don't rush through it. Take a few minutes when you get to the mountain peaks of the story to just look around. When David is crowned under the golden sun of Hebron, take a minute to think back to Genesis 3:15. When God promises that he's going to make a new covenant with his people, take a moment to *feel* what that promise would have meant to a people whose tears were still being soaked up by foreign soil. When Jesus dies on the cross and the curtain in the temple rips in two, take a minute—look back over the mountains—and imagine the angel with his flaming sword in Eden, barring the way back to God's presence, now sheathing that sword once and for all. Ultimately, stand in awe at God's mercy and greatness. Be astonished at all he did—though he was obligated to do none of it—to save his people from their sins.

Finally, and above all, let the experience of reading the Bible teach you to see Jesus more clearly and therefore worship him more deeply. After all, the whole grand narrative is ultimately about him, and as you see all its themes find their end and goal in him, your vision of him will go 3D. You'll see him not just as a teacher or a good man, or even just as a flat two-dimensional Savior. Rather, you'll see him as the author and perfecter of our faith—the divine and resurrected King who, by his shed blood, inaugurated a new covenant for his people and won access for them back into the presence of God their Creator.

And so, off we go. With joyful anticipation and beating hearts, let's set off on this grand adventure of experiencing the epic story of the Bible!

General Index

abad, 68, 117
Abraham, 45, 46, 47, 53, 69–70,
    87, 120, 125, 133, 143–44,
    145–46, 164
Adam
    covenant with, 85–92
    kingship of, 116–19, 135–36
    rebellion of, 142
    responsibility of, 41–42, 67–69
Adonijah, 126
adultery, 55, 126
Ahaz, 130
Amon-Re, 99
ancient Near East, 95–96
antiquity, 31, 32
apostles, 28–32
ark of the covenant, 126
Artaxerxes, 78
Asa, 129
ascension, 81, 111
Assyria, 101, 106, 130, 154
authority
    of apostles, 28–32
    in creation, 116, 118
    of Christ, 136–37

Baal, 144, 146
Babylon, 101, 107, 130
Balaam, 121, 123
Bathsheba, 126

Bible
    basic structure of, 20–21
    ending of, 59–60
    epic story of, 162–63, 165
    reading of, 14–15, 20, 33, 37, 39,
        64, 83, 161, 164, 165
    storyline of, 37
biblical theology, 64–65
Boaz, 50
Brooks, Max, 21–22
Brown, Dan, 23–24
Buddhism, 19, 20
burnt offering, 150

Cain, 119, 143
Canaan, 48, 94
canonization
    of New Testament, 28–33
    of Old Testament, 24–28
chaos, 49, 122
Chemosh, 144, 146
cherubim, 77
church, 57–59, 81, 162
circumcision, 97
conquest, 47–49
Constantine, 23–24
consummation, 41
contradictions, 162–63
covenant
    with Abraham, 93–98, 99,
        101–2, 105, 106, 108

Scripture Index

Also Available from Greg Gilbert

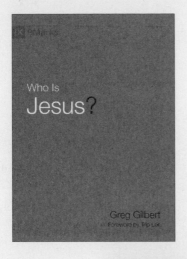

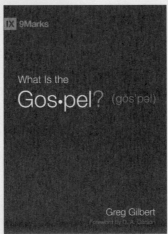

For more information, visit **crossway.org**.